The Digital Jo

MW01231885

Aka Deep W
Comms, Counter-surveillance, Search

*

By Alan Pearce
*

ISBN: 9781521169988
v 0:7b

www.alanpearce.com

"The work of journalism has become immeasurably harder than it ever has been in the past.

"Journalists have to be particularly conscious about any sort of network signaling, any sort of connection, any sort of license plate reading device that they pass on their way to a meeting point, any place they use their credit card, any place they take their phone, any email contact they have with the source - because that very first contact, before encrypted communications are established, is enough to give it all away." *— Edward Snowden 17 July 2014 in The Guardian*.

Table of Contents

3

Navigating the Dangerous Cyber Jungle

Online media safety is of the highest importance to the International Federation of Journalists. After all, the victims are often our members.

The IFJ is the world's largest organization of journalists and our focus is on ways and means to stop physical attacks, harassment and the killing of journalists and media staff. In an age where journalism – like everything else in modern life – is dominated by the Internet, online safety is emerging as a new front.

In this new war, repressive regimes now keep a prying eye on what journalists say, write and film. They want to monitor contacts and they want to suppress information. For journalists, this has become a dangerous game of cat and mouse.

Journalists are on notice – "everything you say and write will be taken down and used to track you and your contacts down."

This merciless pursuit for control of online communications has considerably raised the stakes in the current safety crisis facing journalists and the media. We are living at a time of unprecedented levels of violence against the Press.

Now we need to master the skills necessary to navigate this dangerous cyber jungle.

'Deep for Web Journalists' is the tool to achieve that. This engaging book by Alan Pearce charts a path to online knowledge which should be compelling reading for all journalists.

It offers an uncompromising diagnosis of the perils of online communications and should shatter the confidence many of us place in the unguarded ways of working online.

This book offers simple advice to cover our tracks online and ensure that journalists are not an easy target for online press freedom predators.

Jim Boumelha,
President, *International Federation of Journalists*

Introduction

Journalism has been transformed by the Internet and the Internet has opened journalists to levels of surveillance that would have horrified George Orwell. All journalists should be aware of the dangers they face in the digital world – the emerging battleground.

Being a journalist in 2017 is more dangerous than it ever was. In addition to the usual threats, beatings, murders and war casualties, we are now being actively targeted online by intelligence agencies, law enforcement and others.

These days it is not just journalists working in repressive regimes that need worry. We now know that the US and its cyber-allies – Britain, Canada, Australia and New Zealand – actively monitor domestic journalists in their mass surveillance of the Internet.

Edward Snowden has warned journalists that they are special targets and he has expressed surprise that news organizations rarely have any counter-measures in place.

They harvest our contacts and monitor our telephone logs. They read our emails and texts. They follow our every move online and they keep tabs on every line we write.
But it is not just intelligence agencies and law enforcement that we should worry about. All kinds of people have a vested interest in knowing about your next story – individual criminals and criminal organizations, political parties and extremist groups, law firms and the corporate giants.

This book will show how to block intruders, set up secure communications, mask your identity online and browse and download anonymously, and store any amount of data without leaving a trace.

Deep Web for Journalists "offers an uncompromising diagnosis of the perils of online communications and should shatter the confidence many of us place in the unguarded ways of working online," says Jim Boumelha, President of International Federation of Journalists in his Foreword to the book.

Washington monitors domestic journalists under the National Operations Center's Media Monitoring Initiative and other US agencies are now targeting foreign journalists following recent amendments to the Foreign Intelligence Surveillance Act. Information is regularly shared with foreign agencies and the private sector.

Any US-owned "remote computing service" – meaning any public computer storage or processing service – is open to scrutiny by US intelligence agencies without the need for a warrant.

Start researching sensitive subjects or visiting extremist websites and a tracking device will quickly be planted in your computer to follow you around and report back. It is all too easy for an algorithm to misconstrue your browsing activities and for alarm bells to be set off.

Mobile devices are not secure unless you make them so. If somebody wants to know where you are at this precise moment, your smartphone will tell them – even if it is turned off.

Not every journalist needs be concerned about this. But it is important to know how to operate securely should you ever need to. If you can't offer confidentiality, you are compromised.

So how can we safeguard our sources and communicate without being overheard? How can we conduct sensitive research without having to watch our backs?

In Britain and many other countries the police demand access to *all* their stored data. If they don't hand over passwords to encrypted files they face a lengthy jail term.

This book will show how to overcome these threats without any real technical skills. Using freely downloadable programs and apps, you can block intruders, mask your identity online, set up secure communications and transfer and store any amount of data without anyone being any the wiser.

But to do this we need to employ the black arts. When governments say they must have access to all our computer data to thwart terrorists, pedophiles, money-launderers and drug barons, they are not telling the whole truth. Only the most hapless terrorist is going to give anything away in an email. The seriously bad guys, as a rule, use the Deep Web.

Alan Pearce
April 2017

What is the Deep Web and why is it useful to Journalists?

Simply put, the Deep Web encompasses everything that the conventional search engines can't find. Google may index around 15 billion pages but it only seeks out those that want to be found or have conventional addresses that end in *.com* or *.org*, etc. It skims the surface and offers up the most popular results.

Largely unnoticed by most users, the Internet has been quietly evolving into a vast un-indexed data store. As a result, this Deep Web is so mind-bogglingly huge – some say more than 5,000 times the size of the Surface Internet – that it is both easy to get lost and to stay hidden.

Within this Deep Web are an unknown number of hidden networks; one of which is Tor, a dark world of anonymity. Here, people may communicate secretly and securely away from the attention of governments and corporations, scrutinize top secret papers before WikiLeaks gets them, and discuss all manner of unconventional topics.

Ironically, Tor – which stands for The Onion Router – was set up with funds from the US Navy at the start of the Millennium as a means of covert communication, and later to aid human rights activists inside repressive regimes. But so dark and murky is it, that other agencies now use it, as do most serious criminals.

Tor has its own websites, chat rooms, forums, blogs, file hosts, social networks and other features of the Surface Web. It is very easy to run into arms dealers, drug cartels, spies, pedophiles, kidnappers, slave traders and extremists.

You can buy top grade marijuana direct from the grower, trade stolen credit cards, buy the names and addresses of rape victims, or arrange the murder of an inquisitive reporter or pernickety judge – and then pay for it all with the Deep Web's own currency, the untraceable BitCoin.

Generally, this is why the Deep Web has a bad reputation. But it has positive aspects, too. There are many journalists who use Deep Web tools to communicate securely with whistle blowers and dissidents. Aid agencies use the same techniques to keep their staff safe inside of authoritarian regimes.

The Deep Web is also a largely-unknown research and information resource, a goldmine of knowledge lodged in the databases of academic institutions, small businesses and corporations, research establishments, galleries and governments. If you know the right entry points, you can mine a rich seam of multimedia files, images, software and documents that you cannot find on the Surface Web.

How Intelligence Gathering Works

While some people believe the Internet has set them free, others are waking up to the fact that we are all voluntarily plugged into the finest surveillance apparatus ever devised.

But let's be clear about this: everything we do in the digital world is open to scrutiny by suspicious minds because that's the way intelligence agencies and others work. If they didn't make use of this amazing opportunity, they wouldn't be very good at their job.

All sophisticated security services monitor Internet traffic within their own countries. The US monitors *all* Internet traffic if it passes through US-owned 'processing services', which the bulk of it does. Legally, just the bare bones of the communications are monitored – the who sent what and when, the so-called meta-data.

But, although they may not be open about this, many agencies are now looking directly into the message itself, looking for the expected and the unexpected in all our online communications and activities.

But don't suppose actual agents are used for such mundane tasks. Algorithms of stunning complexity analyze literally every word. And, when certain triggers are pulled, the surveillance moves up a notch and so on until it enters the physical world.

According to the US Government Accountability Office, back in 2004 there were 199 separate data mining programs being run by 16 Federal agencies on the look-out for suspicious activity.

By 2010, *The Washington Post* concluded after a two-year investigation that there were around 1,200 government agencies and 1,900 private companies working on counter-terrorism, homeland security and other domestic intelligence programs from within thousands of secret data processing sites and "fusion centers" that constitute an "alternative geography of the United States".

According to the US government's most recent figures, 4.8 million people now have security clearance that allows them to access all kinds of personal information, while 1.4 million people have Top Secret clearance.

The National Security Agency intercepts and stores the data from billions of emails and other communications, plus one billion phone calls, each day in its attempts to predict wrong-doing in what is termed the "paradigm of prevention" or "predictive policing"; and each day more than 1,600 people have their names added to the FBI's terrorism watchlist.

The US National Counterterrorism Center collects information on *every* US citizen and mines it for terrorism indicators. It then passes on much of this data to other government agencies and increasingly to contractors and corporations.
Agencies like the CIA collect all the data they can and then they store it indefinitely. If they ever need to join the dots, it helps to have all the dots from the past to draw upon. This means that they can go back in time and listen in on 'phone calls made way before the target was ever under suspicion.

Journalists are especially interesting. They have contact with politicians and activists, they have their finger on the pulse and they are capable of causing all kinds of trouble both to governments and to corporations.

If they become interested in you, they will monitor all your online activities and read your email. They will see who your contacts are and they will start to monitor them, too.

Tracking people in cyberspace is child's play, especially when more than half of all Internet users have a page on Facebook. Big Data – Social, Mobile and Cloud – has altered the flow of information, overtaking traditional media. With commercially-available software like Raytheon's social media data mining tool RIOT, simply enter a person's name and up pops a colorful graph showing where they have been, who they met and what they all look like. It then predicts their future movements.

If they have someone in their sights, the bad guys then insert malware into the smartphone or computer and take remote control; listening in on conversations, intercepting SMS and VoIP calls, and noting everything. They also harvest the contacts and monitor them, too, along with everyone that they know.

Nothing escapes their attention. There is a school of thought that the most successful companies got where they are today with a little outside help.

Imagine starting a service where millions of people will openly detail their lives and speak their minds. Then imagine being approached by an organization that would like to help you become a global brand. All you have to do in return is add a 'backdoor' allowing them direct access to the real names, physical addresses and activity logs of everybody who signs up.

If you don't play ball, well, your business will go nowhere and you might find that suddenly your credit cards don't work and then things begin to spiral downwards for you. It's not really an option. You build a backdoor. That's the theory.

When Briton Leigh Van Bryan, 26, planned a vacation to Hollywood, he tweeted friends that he intended to "destroy America", meaning in London-slang that he was going to have a jolly good time.

The Department of Homeland Security didn't see it that way and were ready and waiting for him when he landed at Los Angeles Airport. He was handcuffed, interrogated for hours, locked in the cells overnight and unceremoniously deported.

They knew everything about him except what he was actually talking about. Algorithms may be smart but they just don't get the nuances. It's the little things like this which can set a suspicious mind off on a very deep investigation or drag you quickly off to a window-less cell.

It's the same with email. If you don't believe that every word you write is scrutinized, try typing into an email the words, *bomb kill Obama Tuesday* and see how long it takes for them to come and get you.

The emails you receive can be equally dangerous. Anything that contains an image or link in HTML format, not to mention attachments, could result in a tracking device, key-logger or a beacon being inserted into your device, alerting the sender to your presence and precisely where you are sitting at this very moment.

Trackers are everywhere. Pay a visit to Twitter or Facebook and they will instantly plant little robots that follow you around, noting everything you do. It is also understood that the NSA 'piggy-backs' on the cookies of the big companies, drawing data directly from Google users and others.

To scoop up everybody else, the agencies channel users through a series of 'black boxes' or inspection points scattered around the net which then read everything that passes through them, analyzing it, logging it, storing it for deeper examination, or marking it for further attention.

With this so-called Deep Packet Inspection (DPI), all Internet traffic can be read, copied or modified, as can websites. DPI can also see who is uploading or downloading, what is inside and who is looking for it.

Websites can be blocked and so can specific items within sites such as a particular video on
Generally, ISPs and most governments can examine the 'header' of a message, seeing where it came from and where it's going, but they have not been able legally to peer inside. DPI has been used for years in the commercial world but only Tunisia, China, Iran and Kazakhstan legally use the system to curb dissidents.

However, under the Foreign Intelligence Surveillance Act, the NSA and FBI are legally able to tap directly into the servers of any US Internet company and one of the best ways to do that is with DPI. Under the PRISM program, the NSA is apparently able to access the servers of at least nine leading US providers, including Google, Facebook and Microsoft. The companies themselves would not necessarily know that they had been compromised.

But this is small-fry. The US – along with its Five Eyes cyber-partners Britain, Canada, Australia and New Zealand – taps directly into undersea and fiber optic cables as well as communications satellites, taking the data from the source. The result is that virtually everything which travels on the Surface Internet, and much else, is open to inspection.

The Community Comprehensive National Cybersecurity Initiative Data Center in Utah, code-named Bumblehive, is now on-stream, capturing all communication globally, including the complete contents of private emails, cell phone calls and Internet searches, plus all the personal data trails from parking receipts, bank transfers, travel itineraries and bookstore purchases.

Data storage is remarkably cheap and getting cheaper every year. Analyzing and storing it all is now a cost-effective reality and, once again, they would be failing as intelligence agencies if they didn't. The CIA proudly admits that "it is nearly within our grasp to compute on all human generated information."

Today everything is connected, everything communicates and everything is a sensor. Technology is moving so fast that even the major agencies can't keep up. Put all these things together and the inanimate becomes sentient and capable of decision-making. Suddenly the great dystopian fear is a reality.

And this is how they profile us all. It's been happening for years in the commercial world. Only when you appear to step out of line, say the wrong thing or spend too long looking at a bad kind of wiki, will you become interesting to the suspicious minds.

But mistakes are easily made in a world overseen by computers and not so easily rectified, as Mikey Hicks of New Jersey knows well. Every time he tries to fly, he is detained and thoroughly searched. Mikey is 12 years old and has been on an Airline Watch List since he was two.

As it turns out, the bad guys don't say *kill* or *bomb* in their emails or on Twitter. The terrorists and super-criminals can also hire the smartest brains in the IT world, and they pay better.

According to the US National Academy of Sciences, whilst data mining may work in the commercial world, it simply isn't feasible to prevent atrocities because terrorists don't use a one size fits all model; they change and adapt their *modus operandi* as they go along, preventing the algorithms from picking out a pattern.

Curiously, governments and intelligence agencies know this, too.

How this affects Journalists

All journalists should be aware of the dangers they face in the digital world – the emerging battleground.

A reporter working on a story about a local man with an idea to counter IEDs (improvised explosive devices) would very likely read up on military statistics, watch a few explosions on YouTube, check out the different detonators and view an extremist website or two. He would be asking for trouble.

From that day on, the reporter would be a marked man or woman. They could no longer research in private or correspond in confidence. They would never be able to protect the anonymity of a source.

What they could have done, however, was install a few free, tried and tested programs and tweak their computer and smartphone. They could easily have masked their identity and location. And they could ask questions without Google or the NSA building a profile on them.

But it is not just intelligence agencies and law enforcement that we should worry about. All kinds of people have a vested interest in knowing about your next story – individual criminals and criminal organizations, political parties and extremist groups, law firms and the corporate giants.

Large business interests have their own intelligence units. They know what is being said about them and by whom. They keep track of their competitors and they know when somebody starts asking awkward questions about them.

If big business wanted to destroy a journalist's reputation this is simplicity itself. It would be a small matter to fill the reporter's computer with images of child sexual abuse and then tip off the local police anonymously. No one would ever take the reporter seriously again. Even their closest friends and family would turn against them.

So be warned. The Internet is a dangerous place and there are people out there with high-end computer skills who can seriously damage your life.

The key is not to attract attention in the first place by learning to operate beneath the radar. And if you suspect you are being monitored there are ways and means of hiding your activities and communicating in ways that cannot be discovered or intercepted.

But it is also vitally important not to "go quiet". If you suspect you are being observed, you must carry on as you have always done. Continue buying cinema tickets online, chatting with your friends and posting to the social media, and all the rest of it.

When US Navy SEALS killed Osama bin Laden, they knew his was the only house in Abbottabad that did not have broadband or connect to any phone network. He did not have a Facebook page and he never tweeted his friends. And this is what gave him away.

So you must give them something to monitor. You need to keep them satisfied and to divert their attention while you operate elsewhere in unexpected ways.

And, rather like spies in a James Bond movie, journalists have an array of digital tools to call upon, both to mask their identity and to provide real confidence that their correspondence, notes and contacts are secure.

There are smartphone apps that let you see in the dark or measure the height of a building. You can film and record without being rumbled; send emails, Private Messages and text messages that cannot be intercepted or read, and you can make secure, encrypted VoIP calls.

With any modern device you can access banned websites and take over and control public and private security cameras. You can continue tweeting when the authorities take down Twitter locally. You can pass on and store documents away from prying eyes. You might even hide news footage of a massacre inside a music track on your iPod while you slip across the border.

In the old East Germany under the Stasi Secret Police people didn't talk openly because they didn't know who was listening. And now we have the same situation on the Internet. And the ability to speak openly was one of the best things about the Internet. In many ways – with their suspicious minds – they've ruined something that was truly marvellous.

So, will people speak openly if they know they're being monitored? Is this likely to have an effect on the free flow of thought and ideas? The answer can only be "Yes".

In short, free democratic society is threatened by this mass surveillance. And the Press – as the cornerstone of democracy – has never been so threatened before.

It's time to wake up to the Internet and to see it as the 21st century battleground where, in many ways, we're all combatants.

And, for the first time, we're combatants in a war not simply observers – not simply trying to get at the truth but actual targets in the sights of "democratic" governments and not just those of the repressive regimes, those that have traditionally tried to silence the Press and stamp on the Human Spirit.

The Internet may be an amazing tool. But, if we don't learn to master it, it may be the end of us all. Because if we can't work in private and offer confidentiality then we are compromised.

And then what future this profession?

A technical aside

We are living in a constantly-changing game of cat and mouse. Techniques that might work today might not work tomorrow.

In the brief period since this book was first published, a number of groups offering cyber-security and counter-surveillance technology have been forced out of business or outright compromised.

We endeavor to keep this book as up-to-date as possible. If, however, you find that any of the techniques offered here are no longer valid, please let us know as soon as possible so we can launch an update.

Deep Web links given in this book and marked <!> can only be opened in a Tor-Firefox browser, which you will learn to configure later.

Free, open source software is generally preferable to the paid-for variety because it can be tested by developers and any logging devices or backdoors can be identified. All proprietary encryption software should be treated with caution.

If you suspect that you may be a target, never make Internet purchases of digital devices – smartphones, laptops, tablets, computer hardware, memory cards or even USB leads.

There are credible reports that items destined for specific targets are being intercepted in the mail and that key-loggers and other malware are being installed directly into the devices (sometimes even injection-molded into the frame). Wherever practical, make purchases from physical stores and try to pay cash.

Be alert that no single system or piece of software is 100% secure or safe. However, by combining the techniques in the following pages, it is possible to operate in such a way that nobody ever need know.

Do not rely on the technology itself to keep you safe. You need to devise tactics and strategies to avoid being found in the first place. This book will show you how.

PART 1 – Security

If you are conducting sensitive research or just your normal day-to-day activities, it is advisable to make a few, simple adjustments to your computer.

Setting up Defenses
Browser — arguably the most security-conscious browsers are Comodo's IceDragon for those who like Mozilla's Firefox and Comodo Dragon for those more familiar with the Google Chrome browser. Mac users should opt for Firefox.

You can switch between regular and private browsing by opening the settings. This will prevent your computer from logging your activities but it will not make you invisible. While Mozilla Firefox has a large number of free add-ons to help you beef up security, IceDragon has the edge.

Spend a few seconds tweaking with the browser *Settings*.
- Select *Options/Privacy.* Tick the option *Do not tell sites anything about my tracking preferences*.
- Under *Advanced/Network* tick *Tell me when a website asks to store data for offline use*.

Install the following free add-ons to improve security:
- **Force HTTPS** — Hypertext Transfer Protocol Secure (HTTPS) is used for secure end-to-end communication. HTTPS Finder for Firefox automatically detects and enforces HTTPS connections when available, providing a reasonable guarantee that you are communicating with the intended website and not an imposter, plus ensuring that communications between the user and site cannot be read or forged by a third party. The Electronic Frontier Foundation has its own free version HTTPS Everywhere for Firefox, IceDragon and Chrome browsers.

- **Kill Trackers** — **Blur** (formerly Do Not Track Me) blocks web beacons and trackers that monitor browsing habits. Once installed, a tiny icon in the top right corner issues an alert whenever a site has a bead on you. Twitter and Facebook, for example, will try to insert trackers that follow you all over the Internet, allowing them to build a detail profile of your movements and interests. If people ever wonder how the social networks make money, this is how. There is also Disconnect Me which additionally offers a secure search facility.

- **Control Cookies** — **BetterPrivacy** allows you to remove or manage cookies and gives various ways to handle Flash-cookies set by Google, YouTube, eBay and others. **Privacy+** does much the same thing. Flash plugins run independently of your browser and bypass any proxy configurations. If you were trying to mask your identity, these will reveal your IP address which in turn will point to your physical address.

- **Java Switch** — **QuickJava** allows you to quickly enable and disable Java, JavaScript and other intrusive plugins which track your location, travels and preferences. Other options include **NoScript** and **Ghostery**.

- **Cache Control** — the **Empty Cache Button** adds a button to Firefox allowing you to quickly empty your browser cache should anyone start looking over your shoulder and optionally reload your page with just one click.

- **Avoid Detours** — to stop websites opening other pages on your browser and taking you off to potentially harmful sites, try **Redirect Remover** which prevents redirects from links and images. Another good option is **RequestPolicy**.

- **Control Ads** — **Adblock Plus** allows you to block online ads from anyone you would rather not hear from. You can choose from a predefined list and you can personalize your own, but don't block sites you use regularly. Amazon, for example, is so stuffed with ads that by switching them off, the site instantly turns to text-only. You can also customize the settings to remove the annoying ads at the beginning of streaming videos on YouTube and elsewhere.

- **Block Baddies** — use either the free or paid-for versions of **AVG** or **Avast** which both warn of and block viruses and spyware entering your machine from malicious websites or the paid-for version of **MalwareBytes** (also see **Keeping out the Spies**).

- **Secure Download** — **DownThemAll** uses the browser's safety settings and so requires no configuration and features an advanced accelerator that speeds things up considerably. You can pause and resume downloads. It also allows you to download all the links or images on a webpage and customize the search criteria. It offers the ability to download a file from different servers at the same time for additional security. **Privoxy** is a web proxy service that fetches items (webpages, images, movies, etc) and passes them on to you when complete.

- **Encrypt** — **Encrypted Communication** encrypts messages prior to transmission, including posts to Facebook and other social networks, and is simpler than many other encryption options.

Search Engines — obviously, Google keeps detailed records of your search queries so select an engine which won't store your records. Options include the Secret Search Labs **engine, DuckDuckGo** and **iXQuick**.

Tighten Router — change the password on the home or office router to prevent unauthorized access. See manufacturer's website for instructions.

Wear a Mask — you can't beat cloaking your identity as one of the safest of all strategies. This way no one need know who or where you are. The simplest solution for quick, anonymous browsing is to use a facility such as **AllNetTools**, **Guardster** or **Anonymouse**.

These free services allow you to type in any web address and then travel around without leaving a trace of your activities or giving away your location. These are particularly useful for sensitive search engines queries and for visiting locally banned websites.

You can set up a proxy – which gives the impression that you are in another place – by fiddling with the *Settings* and changing the IP address to one provided by **Proxy4Free** or **Rosinstruments** but this can slow your machine down. A simpler solution is **Stealthy**, an add-on which seeks out the fastest proxies available and automatically routes you through them.

A more secure alternative is a Virtual Private Network (VPN), effectively a 'secret tunnel' where all your online activities are screened from the service provider and eavesdroppers. Free versions include **FreeVPN** and **ProXPN**. A popular and fast paid-for option is **VyprVPN** which also speeds things up, too.

Regularly backup all data, either to a separate storage device or to a Cloud service you can trust, options include **Tresorit** and **Seafile**.

Avoid keeping sensitive data on your computer; store separately.

If it's not too late, never post any personal information – birth dates, family connections, location, travel plans, identifying photographs, etc – on the social networks.

It is always a good idea to cover the forward-facing camera on any device because you can never be certain if somebody is watching or not.

All this is good for general activity on the Surface Web but it is not 100% secure.

It is safe to assume that if law enforcement or the intelligence agencies want to monitor anybody's Internet access – read their emails and social media postings, harvest their contacts, find out what they are searching for and downloading, and listen in to their calls – then they can, regardless of the niceties of court orders and warrants.

This means that absolutely everything is open to inspection.
In the final scene of the movie "Raiders of the Lost Ark", they place the Ark of the Covenant inside a crate and then they hide it inside a humungous warehouse full of identical crates. This is the principle by which to operate, but on an infinitely vaster scale – down in the Deep Web.

Don't think of a needle in a haystack. Think of a needle in a universe of haystacks.

1.2 Accessing Hidden Networks

Tell someone that you know how to go off-radar on the Internet and as a rule they won't believe you. They imagine the intelligence agencies have state-of-the-art technology and can see everything you do. This is only partially true.

They do have amazing technology but they can only see things if they know where to look. Down in the Deep Web, by mixing and matching different technologies, you can stay out of sight and make it seriously difficult for any adversary to locate you.

There are several hidden networks. There may be hundreds but nobody knows for sure. We are going to access the most user-friendly – Tor.

First you need a specially-configured web browser to divert your traffic through a worldwide volunteer network of servers. This conceals your location and your activities, effectively hiding you among all the other users. Tor works by encrypting and re-encrypting data multiple times as it passes through successive relays. This way the data cannot be unscrambled in transit.

Tor does have its flaws and should not be considered completely safe. Although your IP address is concealed, a digital fingerprint can linger allowing someone accessing your local network – a Wi-Fi provider or an ISP working with criminals or law enforcement – to glean some idea of your activities.

An option here is to first configure a VPN service to route all your traffic through a 'secret tunnel' and then activate the Tor-Firefox browser. This will also prevent an eavesdropper seeing that the Tor network has been accessed.

The waters can be further muddied by requesting more than one site at a time or by downloading more than one item simultaneously, and by regularly re-setting the *Use a new identity* facility on the Tor control panel.

Certain plug-ins will not work on the Tor browser such as Flash, RealPlayer and QuickTime as they can be manipulated into revealing an IP address. Close down other browsers while you access Tor and disconnect or cover your webcam lens.

Begin by searching online and downloading the free **Tor-Firefox bundle**. This is safe and easy to install. Simply follow the on-screen instructions and a gateway to the Deep Web can be configured in minutes with no special skills.

Be absolutely certain that you are downloading from the **torproject.org** website. A hidden network used in Iran was recently infiltrated when a fake version of their modified browser was distributed which gave away the identity of users.

Also be sure to keep the Tor browser up-to-date. A warning sign will appear on the start page if you need to update. Once loaded, the browser will display a very basic-looking webpage (the Deep Web resembles the Surface Web circa 1996) and the words:

> *Congratulations. This browser is configured to use Tor.*
> *You are now free to browse the Internet anonymously.*

You are now anonymous and free to explore Tor or branch off to the Surface Web with minimal risk of being monitored.

To tighten security further, employ some form of end-to-end encryption while browsing or messaging. You will find various options in the following pages. Also add on to the Tor browser **HTTPS Everywhere**, **Blur** and the secure downloader **Down Them All**.

If you are in a country where ISPs or the government block the Tor network, open *Settings* on the Tor control panel, select *Network*, and then tick the box *My ISP blocks connections to the Tor network*. You are now given the option to *Add a Bridge* or *Find Bridge Now*. If no bridges (non-public relays) are found, go to the Tor bridge relay page on the Surface Web and select them manually by cutting and pasting until you find one that works for you. Add as many bridges as possible as this increases your chances of connecting and improves security.

Using Tor

Rather like time travel, this level of the Internet appears much as it did in the very early days, including the lengthy wait while pages load. There are no frills or flashy graphics, just simple text and images.

On Tor, people communicate secretly and securely. Whistle blowers and dissidents, activists and journalists, aid-workers and academics, criminals and terrorists, and rather a lot of librarians, all carry on their day-to-day activities.

Top secret papers are posted here, as are guides and wikis for every type of activity, legal and otherwise; and all manner of unconventional views are expressed. Here you can lurk hidden and surreptitiously store any amount of data for free.

This is pioneer territory with very few settlers; perhaps 400,000 daily users at best compared to the 2 billion plus who stay up top. Some of the natives are hostile because they would rather keep the place to themselves. Others are friendly because they know more users mean more people to hide amongst.

Deep Websites can disappear or fail to load from time to time. If you have difficulty opening a particular page, just try again later and it may reappear.

The Tor Network is not an easy place to search, however, the **Onion City** search engine has a very good try.

Entry Points

Recent activity by various government agencies, mostly in the USA and the UK, has seen a number of Hidden Services on Tor disappear. These are likely to return in one form or another. Those listed here were active at time of publication.

- The Hidden Wiki <!>
  http://kpvz7ki2v5agwt35.onion/wiki/index.php/Main_Page
  often described as the hub of the Deep Web, this is the best starting point for new-comers. Here you can find lists of other hidden networks and links to black market goods and financial services, file hosts, blogs, forums, political groups and whistle-blowing boards. Beware that many of the traders here are pure scammers, so be very cautious before parting with any money. The more reliable operators have attached forums where people can discuss the services. The wiki is available in 17 languages. Mirror sites: <!> http://wikitjerrta4qgz4.onion/ and <!> http://zqktlwi4fecvo6ri.onion/wiki/index.php/Main_Page. The Uncensored Hidden Wiki can be found at <!> http://kpvz7kpmcmne52qf.onion/wiki/index.php/Main_Page
- TorLinks <!> torlinkbgs6aabns.onion links directory where you can add your own links and set up a Deep Website.
- OnionDir <!> http://dirnxxdraygbifgc.onion/ Tor link directory.
- OnionList <!> http://jh32yv5zgayyyts3.onion/ Onion link list and directory.
- TorBlog <!> http://thehiddenwiki.org/blog/ Updates on Tor activity.
- ParaZite Links List <!> http://kpynyvym6xqi7wz2.onion/links.html
- Onion URL Repository <!> http://32rfckwuorlf4dlv.onion/

- TorWiki <!> http://torwikignoueupfm.onion/index.php?title=Main_Page
- All Your Bases <!> http://3fyb44wdhnd2ghhl.onion/ simple link launch pad.
- HackForum <!> a2emrmdsprmm6t7i.onion/index.php hacker's bulletin board.

Deep Search Engines <!> — Tor has a number but none are in any way comprehensive:
- **The Abyss** http://nstmo7lvh4l32epo.onion
- **Deepsearch** http://hpuuigeld2cz2fd3.onion/
- **Torch** http://xmh57jrzrnw6insl.onion/
- http://3g2upl4pq6kufc4m.onion/ – DuckDuckGo Search Engine
- Onion City Deep Search engine accessible on the Surface Web.

Many more Onion links can be found by visiting **www.deepdotweb.com**.

1.3 Secure Communications

People communicate on the hidden networks in much the same way as they do on the regular Internet. Personal messaging and texting are likely to overtake email as the preferred form of communication and this is reflected on Tor.

Email — use Tor or a VPN and sign up anonymously with a web-based free email service. Always remember to log-out at the end of the session. The Hidden Wiki has a detailed and current list of email providers recommended by Tor users <!> **http://zqktlwi4fecvo6ri.onion/wiki/Email**.

Email can also be encrypted within the message, along with any attachments, but this in itself may draw attention. See **Encryption**. A good, free option is BitMessage Mail Gateway, a Swiss-based Tor email service <!> http://bitmailendavkbec.onion/.

A Surface Web option is **unseen.is**, an Icelandic-based free and subscription service offering 4096-bit encrypted email, chat, VoIP and file sharing. Another secure Swiss-based option is **ProtonMail** created in collaboration with scientists at Harvard, the Massachusetts Institute of Technology and the European research lab CERN.

Most infections come via email so it is advisable to disable the HTML settings because, when opened, they can transmit directly back to the sender or result in malware being planted inside your machine. Generally, you can do this via the *Settings* tab on the website. Look for and untick *Display attachments online* or tick *View message body as plain text*. Be careful with all downloaded attachments. See **Keeping out the Spies**.

If you need to send an email that positively cannot be traced back to you, there are numerous email options, including temporary **10-minute emails** and re-mailing services such as **AnonyMouse**. Re-mailers strip off any codes that identify you and add new ones along a multiple journey. When the email arrives at its destination, it cannot be traced back to you. This, of course, means they cannot reply. However, you can then give them an alternative means of contact.

A very simple option is to open a free email account with a company employing good encryption and privacy such as **unseen.is** and then give the address and log-in details to the other party. Messages are then written but saved as *Drafts* and never sent. The draft messages are then accessed by those with the password. This way the emails are never actually transmitted so are not easily intercepted. Be sure to change addresses regularly as over-active *Draft* boxes can arouse suspicion.

Bitmessage — working on a similar system to **BitCoin**, Bitmessage is a decentralized, peer-to-peer messaging system that allows users to send encrypted messages to another person or to many subscribers. It uses strong authentication which means that the sender of a message cannot be spoofed, and it aims to hide 'non-content' data, like the sender and receiver of messages, from passive eavesdroppers. Still in the beta stage, Bitmessage is simple to install and runs on most operating systems and on smartphones. Also ideal for installing direct to a USB thumb drive, see **Concealed Carry**.

Scramble Calls — one of the best options for secure peer-to-peer telephone and video calling is **Silent Phone** which allows you to make secure encrypted phone calls all over the world, over any network – 3G, 4G and Wi-Fi. Silent Phone connects directly to a custom-built secure network for HD sound and vision quality and utilizes ZRTP Protocol software by Phil Zimmermann, the inventor of PGP encryption. Each subscriber receives a private encrypted 10-digit phone number. Easily integrates existing contacts on your device and works on smartphones and tablets (iPhone, iPad, Android, Galaxy and Nexus). A free alternative is **Jitsi**, an open-source encrypted VoIP service for audio/video and chat that supports protocols such as SIP, XMPP/Jabber, AIM/ICQ, Windows Live, Yahoo! Also, there is **Signal**, a free version of **RedPhone** providing end-to-end encrypted text and VoIP calls for both iOS and Android.

Secret Messaging

- **Otr.to** — very neat browser-based free messaging system for secure p2p chat, self-destructing messages and secure file sharing. Does not work with Tor as it requires JavaScript.
- **Tox.im** — free Surface Web instant messaging and VoIP service that aims to prove a secure alternative to Skype.
- **Sigatnt** <!> http://sigaintevyh2rzvw.onion/ — Dark Net email system that masks identity and location of sender.
- **Heml.is** is a secure messaging system for iPhone and Android from the Swedish Pirate Party.
- **Cryptocat** offers relatively simple encrypted chat for most Surface Web browsers. The latest version also works on Facebook.
- **TorBox** <!> http://torbox3uiot6wchz.onion/ — Hidden email service only accessible via Tor.
- **PrivNote.com** — free Surface Web-based service that allows you to send top secret notes over the Internet. Requires no password or registration. Write a note and it will generate a link. Copy and paste the link into an email or PM and send. The recipient then

clicks the link to see the note in their browser. The note then automatically self-destructs which means no one can read the note again, and the link dies. You can choose to be notified when your note is read.

- **SMS4Tor <!> http://sms4tor3vcr2geip.onion/** — just like PrivNote but on Tor.

- **SpamMimic.com** — free online tool that converts simple messages into *spamtext*, the kind of weirdly-written junk that arrives in everybody's email box and therefore looks totally innocuous. Simply compose a short message, hit the *Encode* button and out comes a load of nonsense which you cut and paste into an email. The recipient then pastes the *spamtext* into the *Decode* box and out comes the original message.

All this will provide a very good level of security but there will still be traces of your activity on the computer. To get around that, we need to take a few tips from James Bond.

1.4 Concealed Carry

To be extra safe, access Tor directly from a USB drive, SD card or portable hard drive. These can be used on any Internet-ready computer. Install Tor/Firefox and other useful programs directly to the device and then encrypt it.

A dialogue box to the drive will open as soon as the device is slipped into a computer. Select *Start Tor Browser* and you will leave no helpful trace of your web journey on the machine and no one should be able to track you.

Sensitive USB drives should be fully encrypted. This is far more effective than encrypting individual files within the drive. When a computer writes data to a USB drive, it uses what's called 'wear leveling', which means it sends data to random parts of the memory to prevent the same information blocks being used repeatedly and wearing out the drive.

As a result, when updated or new data is written to the USB, it can be sent all over the place, including to areas outside of the encrypted area. Equally, eraser programs may not be fully effective if you are just wiping individual files. See **Cleaning Up**.

This means an adversary who can access the drive may also be able to access the unencrypted elements that have been randomly stored. When it comes to clearing data, the entire USB drive should be formatted and erased rather than erasing individual files. There are numerous tools including the open-source **FreeOTFE** which uses on-the-fly encryption, meaning data is automatically encrypted and decrypted without you having to do anything except enter a password. When installed, your USB drive will contain an encrypted volume where you can store sensitive data.

For Mac users, the operating system has a built-in encryption tool. Simply plug in your USB drive and open up *Disk Utility* in the *Utilities* folder inside the *Applications* folder. Here you have a number of encryption options. You can also set the size of the volume, number of partitions and the format. It can be locked by password.

For those that like to run Linux, there is PenDriveLinux, a portable Linux operating system that runs off a USB.

Tricky Tails

Tails, which stands for The Amnesic Incognito Live System, is a free program that comes pre-configured with the Firefox browser, instant messaging, email client, office suite, image and sound editor, etc. However, installation is not for the faint-hearted.

Tails accesses the computer's RAM memory which is automatically erased when the computer shuts down, leaving neither trace of Tails nor your activities, but do read the *Warnings* page to understand the system's limitations.
You initially download an ISO image (archive file) that you later burn to a CD or install directly to a detachable drive. You will need to have set up a **PGP Key** first.

All that said, many people this one just too complex. Luckily, there are simpler alternatives.

Or Keep it Simple

Install the Tor bundle as above and then download the free **PortableApps.com** 'Platform' that bundles together a wide range of recommended open-source portable applications, from text editor to security software. Begin by downloading the **Platform** and then choose from the extensive list of apps. When running, a small dialogue box appears with access to the installed apps and to file storage.

Suggestions include:

- Notepad Portable Text Editor, with support for multiple languages.
- VLC Media Player Portable.
- IrfanView Portable, graphic viewer for Windows. View pictures, vector graphics, animated images, movies, icon files, etc.
- GIMP Portable, Windows image editor.
- Sumatra PDF Portable, lightweight PDF viewer.
- Eraser Portable, securely delete files and data.
- 7-Zip Portable, portable version of **7-Zip**. Works with compressed 7z, ZIP, GZIP, BZIP2, TAR, and RAR files.
- AVG Anti-Virus Free.
- ClamWin Portable.
- McAfee Stinger Portable, common virus and 'fake alert' remover.
- Spybot Search & Destroy Portable, Spyware detection and removal.
- CamStudio Portable screen recorder.
- Command Prompt Portable.
- Download with **DownThemAll**.

Conversely, you might install the PortableApps 'Platform' within a secure Cloud store, and only keep a VPN and Tor on the drive. That way, there is nothing incriminating on your person and you can hand over encryption keys without fear of giving anything away. You just need to memorize the Cloud store location and login – accessing via the Tor browser.

For those that like to run Linux, there is **PenDriveLinux**, a portable Linux operating system that runs off a USB.
Be sure to update software regularly to maintain security levels.

1.5 Hiding Things

Transferring Secret Data

Whenever journalists are arrested, the authorities are quick to remove computers, smartphones and storage devices for examination by forensic investigators. Rather than store sensitive data or contacts on your computer, either keep them on a USB thumb drive or SD card and encrypt, or upload to an online file store or secure Cloud on the Surface Web or within Tor.

On no account use any of the big commercial Cloud data stores as these can often be accessed by US agencies and their commercial counterparts. You could encrypt Cloud data but this may only increase their interest in you.
There are an increasing number of Cloud stores now promising security and anonymity, options include **Tresorit.com** and **Seafile.com**.

It is also important to remove sensitive data from laptops and smartphones, etc, when on assignment and store on a detachable drive or SD card. Or rather, do not travel with sensitive data on your person but upload to a secret file store and access it at your destination.

Individual files, such as text or images, can be placed inside a **RAR** or **7z file** and encrypted. Large files, such as *AVI, DivX*, etc, should be split into several components before uploading. Use **HJSplit**, a free program that both splits and re-joins large files.
For additional security, do not upload all the component parts to the same server/host as they may be spotted and opened. Instead, upload to as many different servers/hosts as possible. Give each part a different name. Remember to rename them in the correct order so they can then be un-split. Do not give the files any name that identifies the content.

Increasingly, many news organizations are employing a system known as **SecureDrop**, from the Freedom of the Press Foundation that allows whistle blowers to send material anonymously. It also incorporates an encrypted messaging service.

Hosting, Storing and Sharing

- **Real Hosting** — <!> **http://hosting6iar5zo7c.onion/** hosting service paid with BitCoin.
- **OneSwarm.org** — P2P file sharer where you can select who to share with.
- **RetroShare** — securely chat and share files using a 'web-of-trust' to authenticate peers and OpenSSL to encrypt communication, plus PMs, forums and other channels.
- **Pastebin.com** — share text on the Surface Web for a set period of time.

Encryption and Cryptography

Contrary to popular belief, the NSA and its cyber partner GCHQ have not broken Internet encryption codes. What they have done is force some commercial encryption companies to install secret 'exploits' such as 'backdoors' into their programs and they have also hacked into various servers to steal encryption codes.

If an intelligence agency were capable of breaking full-on encryption then the mathematical community would soon know about it, and so would we.

Open-source encryption programs and services such as PGP are not likely to be affected and should remain effective.
However, some countries have introduced mandatory key disclosure laws, compelling users to hand over their encryption keys to law enforcement and intelligence agencies on request.

These include Antigua and Barbuda, Australia, Belgium, Canada, Finland, France, India, Poland and the United Kingdom. Additionally, agencies in many other countries may apply extra-judicial pressure on users to disclosure encryption methods and keys.

Data that can be read without special tools is called *plaintext* or *cleartext*. Hiding plaintext is called *encryption*. When plaintext is encrypted it turns to unreadable gibberish and this is called *ciphertext*. When you turn it back to its original plaintext this is called *decryption*.

Email Encryption — unencrypted email can easily be read or altered by someone with access to any of the computers along the route followed by the email. However, be warned that if you are being monitored the fact that you are encrypting your email will ring alarm bells and open you to deeper inspection.

Equally, if someone can access your computer, they may acquire or change your encryption codes, either denying you access or leaving you with the impression that your data is safe. They may also impersonate you and send out bogus messages. Be warned, too, that agencies like the NSA and GCHQ employ systems that seek out encrypted documents which again may open you to inspection.

That said, PGP (Pretty Good Privacy) Public Key Cryptography is a recommended means of scrambling data prior to emailing. However, PGP is not easy to set up and, if you have difficulty, don't take it personally. A study found that most people seriously struggle with even the basics. However, a couple of neat workarounds are shown below.

Created by Philip Zimmermann, PGP is the standard program for secure email and file encryption on the Internet. Originally designed as a human rights tool, PGP was published for free on the Internet in 1991. This put Zimmermann in trouble with the US authorities when PGP spread worldwide and apparently violated US export restrictions for cryptographic software. This is why you will find separate versions for the US market and elsewhere.

It works like this: access any PGP program and with it generate two keys – a public key and a private key. The public key you give out to anyone wanting to send you secure information. The sender uses your public key to encrypt the data and then sends it. When you receive the data, you unscramble it with your private key. It also allows people to securely pass on data without any pre-existing security arrangements.

A typical PGP Public Key looks like this:

-

-----BEGIN PGP PUBLIC KEY BLOCK-----
Version: BCPG C# v1.7.1.0

mI0ET9YJ8wEEAI9MzWz7n8ipl/+owM/LeBON0cSGDpFs2XnVEX6goi//IpEf
aLaZ
8Xedyx0olgKfBinLkH6FCIOMdkXR+0aH1ZIxhT3JteAjweBfSPvEKCakf6P6Zm
FP
G2E5+3nzsv+8HnYfNCJtKNf11+OLFXbFjtLrxyG8SUZ6dLD3v2jA/0d1ABEBAA
G0
EnBncEBhbGFucGVhcmNlLmNvbYicBdBABAgAGBQJP1gnzAAoJEBe21rDUF
USDo9wD
/RvlfoTzM12IFU6aijwHCmZ8vMevydgPAwM4vJ8U8Jt+9rCWtq9V/oO0xLvK
RWuM
1PuTWiuCCtbukViQfVY3rVRyjCNnMYjNGRvb3D6ipbctxguE/KASLZSd7yf5r0
8c
5OXh7LXbsu6bqnjv0fSUdytRXm70dosxDcs/4PglM/UA
=+IH0
-----END PGP PUBLIC KEY BLOCK-----

-

46

There are two free programs that you can run directly from your computer either as a standalone program or as an add-on to your dedicated emailer – visit **www.pgpi.org** – but these can be a little tricky to set up. Equally, those with Windows 64-bit machines may find that many programs freeze or crash.

The Icelandic free email service **unseen.is** has a facility allowing you to send and receive PGP encryption emails with the minimum of complication.

Another simple solution is a free service from Trend Micro. Its **Encryption Client** is a plug-in for Microsoft Outlook that enables secure communications between users. Encrypts emails and attachments with 256-bit AES, the same encryptions standards used by the US government.

Disc Encryption

The safest route for encryption is to encrypt the entire system drive, rather than individual files. Computer forensics can reveal a lot about your computer usage from the system partition including browsing history, bookmarks, emails and contacts details.

Investigators tend to focus heavily on contacts so it is important not only to protect yourself but those you are in contact with. If the investigator cannot access the hard drive their job is so much more difficult.

Steganos Privacy Suite — not free but a very popular, easy-to-use option that locks and encrypts drives or documents and photos, secures USB drives, CDs and DVDs, organizes and manages all passwords and access information, and shreds data so it cannot be reconstructed by recovery applications. Also includes Internet trace destructor.

As a general rule, free, open source programs are more trustworthy than the paid-for varieties.

Free Encryption Software:
- www.kruptos2.co.uk
- www.newsoftwares.net/folderlock
- www.safehousesoftware.com
- www.cypherix.com

Steganography – hiding things inside things

Imagine receiving an email with a harmless photograph of your friend on vacation with her fiancé. But, known only to the two of you, there is a secret message hidden inside the image. This is steganography, the dark cousin of cryptography.

Steganography is the art of writing hidden messages in such a way that no one suspects the existence of the message. It comes from the Greek word *steganos* meaning *concealed writing* and its use goes back to the dawn of time. Think of invisible ink.

These days you can hide almost any kind of digital file by embedding it inside another digital file, such as *a .jpg, bmp* or audio file.

Sensitive footage that needs to be physically smuggled out of a country can be hidden inside a music track on an iPod or smartphone. Secret documents can be embedded inside a photo. Extremists often employ a digital 'drop box' held on a photo within a website to pass instructions on to operatives.
Counter-technology isn't very good and there is little to give the game away unless the file is unexpectedly large. Just looking at the image or trying to open it with a steganalysis program will not show that the image contains any hidden data.

There are many data hiding packages and services available for every operating system. **OpenPuff** from **www.softpedia.com** is a good free program. A good source of information is the Neil Johnson **www.jjtc.com/Steganography/tools.html** website.

Simple messages can be hidden inside photos posted on Facebook with **Secretbook**, a free app for the Google Chrome browser.

Steganos Privacy Suite, as the name might suggest, includes the steganography program *Crypt & Hide* which is simple to use and works like this:

- Open the program and select *New Archive*.
- Add the file to be hidden (think about encrypting it first), click *Save*.
- Next click *Hide* to select a carrier file. Enter a password and save. The program will add the secret document to this image which you can then post. The recipient or viewer will need the same program and password to unlock it.

1.6 Smartphones & Mobile

If you want to be monitored 24/7 and followed wherever you go, buy a smartphone.

Mobile espionage, long the preserve of law enforcement and specialized investigators, has now evolved into a fully-fledged cybercrime industry.

In 2011, Kaspersky Labs detected nearly 5,300 new malicious programs for all mobile platforms. By 2012, the total number of unique malicious files exceeded six million – the vast majority aimed at Android. By 2016, the sheer number out there is hard to quantify.

Mobile devices are also the preferred target of intelligence agencies, with the NSA boasting that it can "own" or control any handset. Technology, as a rule, tends to move forwards in time and not backwards and this is equally true of surveillance technology, so it is a good idea to start collecting older models (known as "burners") and to use them in conjunction with pre-paid sim cards (collected free or paid for with cash) for all sensitive communications.

Threats facing modern devices come in three main forms – SMS Trojans, adware, and exploits to gain control of the device. Smartphones can also be infected when connected to compromised computers and vice versa.

Additionally, law enforcement may oblige the service provider to remotely reprogram a phone's air card allowing for precision tracking. This technique, generically known as 'stingray' or IMSI catcher, allows agents to spoof a legitimate cell tower and trick the smartphone into connecting directly to the stingray.

Anyone using Apple's iOS 7.0.4 and later will find that they can no longer encrypt emails or attachments following some unannounced updates.

The majority of malware comes hidden inside seemingly harmless apps which run in the background and collect data all day long. Malicious programs have been detected in apps on Google Play and the App Store for iOS.

They will track your locations, browsing and downloads, and collaborate with other running apps to build up a detailed profile. Some will intercept incoming calls or activate the microphone. Many apps harvest contacts, some collect passwords, while others send secret messages to premium-rate numbers, running up your charges. Worse still, there are apps that run even when the phone is switched off.

Most apps are free or very cheap because developers make their money by allowing in ad networks and other malevolent parties. Be alert when an app asks permission to use your current location – many don't bother to ask – and never give out email addresses or other personal information.

A growth area in mobile malware is SMS spam where unsolicited messages plant Trojans that hijack the device or just trick users into revealing personal information. As with email and social networks, never open attachments or follow links unless you know them to be safe.

Ironically, viruses are commonly hidden inside smartphone security software. Only install programs from the industry leaders like Comodo, Trend Micro and Kaspersky. For a list of recommended smartphone security apps, visit CTIA www.ctia.org/.

Counter-Intrusion

For Android users, a good free option is **AVG Mobilation** which protects against viruses, malware and spyware. It also identifies unsecure device settings and advises on how to fix them; ensures contacts, bookmarks and text messages are secure; checks media files for malicious software and security threats; guards against phishing; and offers anti-theft protection. Lost or stolen smartphones can be found via Google Maps, plus you can turn your phone's GPS on remotely and have the device send its location to you. You can also lock your phone remotely.

Lookout.com protects iOS or Android devices from unsecure Wi-Fi networks, malicious apps, fraudulent links, etc. You can also use it to back up your contacts by scheduling automatic backups and then accessing the information online, or using it to restore your device in case of a crash or data loss. If you lose your phone, Lookout can locate it on Google Maps – even if the GPS is off and the phone is on silent.

Pry-Fi on Google Play for Android confounds eavesdroppers by putting out a false MAC address. Even if your Wi-Fi is turned off, most modern Android devices will still broadcast your identifying MAC address, announcing who and where you are. According to the developers "Pry-Fi comes with a *War* mode, which when enabled tries to make your Android device appear like dozens of people."

For **iOS**, the Anti-Virus & Malware Scanner does much the same as AVG Mobilation but additionally lets you scan files on remote locations such as Dropbox and web servers. Trend Micro also offers good mobile security for Android.

XPrivacy on Google Play is an open-source Android app that lets you closely control the permissions for each app you install. For example, it can feed your LinkedIn app fake location data or offer Twitter an empty address book while still allowing you to select services you wish to use.

AppLock is a free application lock utility that puts a password-protected lock on all sensitive apps, SMS, contacts, calls, settings, etc. Only available for Android on Google Play.

Do not let your mobile devices out of your sight and this includes leaving them unattended in hotel rooms. If, at airports or border crossings etc, the authorities insist on taking your device away, they may scan the memory or plant malware inside. With laptops and tablets, it is a good idea to place a sticker over any opening parts so you can see if the device has been tampered with.

A very good alternative is to apply a coating of glitter nail polish and then take a photo of it with your smartphone. The glitter in the polish provides a unique pattern that cannot be replicated and which can later be compared to the photo. Additionally, be sure to thoroughly run an anti-spyware program on the device as soon as possible after recovery.

- Put a security code on your smartphone in addition to the SIM code and engage the auto-locking feature.

- Disable network connections and switch off bridging connections. Do not broadcast the Bluetooth device name and disable automated peer-to-peer Wi-Fi connections.

- Turn off Geotagging and GPS location via *Settings > Privacy > Location.* Untick *Use My Location*.

- Whenever possible, access 2G, 3G or 4G networks in preference to free Wi-Fi services.

- Do not store sensitive files on the phone's internal storage. Encrypt data onto the SD card or hide in a secret compartment.

- Enable remote-find or remote-wipe features.

- Do not 'Jailbreak' any device – the act of removing limitations through software or hardware exploits.

- Avoid connecting personal devices to the office network or computer.

- Watch for unauthorized charges, unusual text messages, rapidly-depleting battery and unexpected warmth of the device.

- If you link your smartphone to your car's on-board computer, be sure to regularly delete sensitive information, contacts and travel history.

- Employ a mobile data backup service.

- When covering demonstrations, etc, replace the SD card in the phone with a spare that does not contain personal data and contacts in case of arrest. Also, switch to Airplane Mode to minimize tracking.

- Update models regularly to keep the operating system in line with security enhancements.

- Remove battery or leave your phone behind when meeting contacts, etc. If meeting in a group, do not all remove the battery at the same time as this appears ultra-suspicious to anyone observing any members of the group. The battery cannot be removed from an iPhone but it can be run down until completely flat and then resurrected with a portable battery.

007 Apps

The smartphone in your pocket can easily be turned into a high-tech spy tool and counter-surveillance device to rival anything that Ian Fleming's Q might have dreamt up.

You can secretly record, access banned content and communicate securely, particularly so if used with an unlocked phone and an unregistered pre-paid sim card.

You can take your smartphone onto Tor and keep everything off-radar using apps for Android and iOS with access to both Deep and Surface Webs, plus PM and email without being monitored or blocked. However, you will not be able to access certain sites this way if they insist on JavaScript. Be sure to adjust the security settings as shown above.

In certain situations, such as a demonstrations and riots, Tor-enabled mobiles can still connect to social networks and websites which may be blocked by the government.

However, most social networks make heavy use of JavaScript which will give your identity away but Twitter does have a mobile facility as does Facebook Mobile which do not use JavaScript and can, therefore, be accessed anonymously. Facebook also has a Dark Net presence at **https://facebookcorewwwi.onion**.

Additionally, there is a regular Firefox browser for Android but not for iOS.

- **Scramble Calls —Silent Phone** at https://silentcircle.com/ for Android and iOS provides HD quality securely-encrypted

---

phone/video communication over any network – 2G, 3G, 4G, WiFi. **RedPhone** at www.whispersystems.org offers end-to-end encryption for Android. **Signal** at the same address is a free version of Redphone providing end-to-end encrypted text and VoIP calls for iOS and Android.

- **Secret Messenger** — there are secret messaging systems for all devices. **Secret SMS** for **iOS** will encrypt messages between users and hide them. **Perzo.com** is a new encrypted messaging system for all devices from the people who brought you Skype. There is also **TextSecure** on Google Play for Android. **SureSpot** is an encrypted messaging system for Android and iOS that also allows you to send photos and audio clips. Delete a message and it is also deleted on the recipient's phone. **Telegram** is a free, open-source messaging app for Android and iOS with end-to-end encryption and a self-destruct feature. Also consider **Cyphr**, a 'zero-knowledge' encrypted messaging app. Cyphr generates a unique public and private key pair so only you and the recipient can read the conversation. Available free for Android and iOS from Golden Frog at www.goldenfrog.com,

- **Secret Image** — **Secret Video Recorder Pro** for Android and iOS allows you to seemingly switch off the smartphone while continuing to film. A quick examination of the phone will not show any activity. You can also make and receive calls while the camera is secretly running. **Secret Camera** for iOS allows you to take photos discretely with no shutter sound, preview or immediate playback, while the **Mobile Hidden Camera** does the same for Android. **ReconBot** for Android and iOS is a stealth video recorder that displays a black screen while it records. Includes remote view so you can watch the recording live via a web link. Also includes location data.

- **Remove Image Data** — if you want to upload images that cannot be traced back, you need to remove or alter the EXIF data which most modern cameras implant in the image to give GPS location and other details. Options for Android include the **ExifEraser** and

Exif Wizard for iOS. 'Geotagging' can be turned off in most Android and Apple mobile devices by going into the *Settings*.

- **Secret Audio** — there is the **SC Secret Recorder** for Android. The **Top Secret Audio Recorder** for iOS is a covert recorder that looks like a regular picture-viewing app. You can swipe through the photos but as soon as you tap on an image the recording begins. The recordings can also be password protected.

- **Record Calls** — **Top Secret Call Recorder** for Android and **Call Log Pro** for iOS.

- **Confirm Contacts** — if you receive a call and want to know who actually called, add them to a *Contacts* file and check them out with **Contact Spy** for Android and iOS which lets you quickly search people or companies by running them through this search engine app for web entries, images, news, blogs and US-only physical addresses.

- **Secret Compartment** — secret folders for Android and iOS. Protect sensitive data by storing it in a hidden and encrypted file.

- **Location Trackers** — helpful for dangerous assignments, GPS tracking allows for real-time monitoring of a phone's location via Google Maps. Some, like **GPS Tracking Pro** for Android and iOS, have a check-in feature so you can let the office know you are okay. Also highlights nearby safety points like hospitals.

- **Panic Button** — Amnesty International has introduced an app disguised as a calculator that automatically issues a call for help when the user repeatedly presses the 'On' button, sending SMS distress messages to three previously-set destinations.

- **See in the Dark** — enhanced night vision photography and live feeds with the **Night Vision Camera** for Android and iOS. Works best on cameras with a good-quality lens.

- **Police Scanner** — there are several police and emergency service scanner apps. **Police Scanner** for Android taps into scanners from around the world. For iOS, **Radio Police Scanner** does much the same.

- **Track Planes** — Plane Finder – Live Flight Status Tracker for iOS and Android displays thousands of flights globally using real-time ADS-B signals used by aircraft to transmit their positional data. Enter flight number or tap on the map showing the planes above your head.
- **Chart Vessels** — monitor the position of all manner of vessels from passenger and cargo ships to yachts and gin-palaces. Ship Finder – Live Vessel Tracking for iOS and Android picks up AIS position data from around the world and provides details and photographs of the vessels.
- **Mobile VPN** — to cover your back, there is **HotspotShield.com** which encrypts all smartphone and tablet traffic through a Virtual Private Network (VPN) to mask your identity and prevent tracking. It also allows you to view banned content and access Twitter and Facebook mobile if their services are ever blocked locally.
- **Wipe Clean** — **In The Clear** is an Android app that securely wipes a phone of sensitive data at the click of a button.
- **Remove Evidence** — there are shredders for Android and iOS.
- **Self-Destruct** — perhaps the ultimate weapon in Q's arsenal is the self-destruct feature. The free **Wickr** app at www.mywickr.com allows you to encrypt any data – text, pictures or videos – and then have them self-destruct once unscrambled and viewed, leaving no trace for the forensic investigator. Available for Android and iOS.

1.7 IP Cameras

Modern surveillance cameras use the same technology as any web-enabled device to stream video directly onto a network and, if you know the IP address, you can access the camera on a smartphone or any Internet computer.

Curiously, many cameras are not password-protected; this is especially true of those on private property which often provide street views. Some even have Pan Tilt Zoom functionality which allows anyone to zoom in and out and move the camera around.

To access a specific camera you need to know its IP address, which will look something like this http://82.23.141.150:8080/ or this http://cyclops.sunderland.ac.uk/view/index.shtml and find that you can take full control of the security cameras.

A quick Google search will provide live views of cities globally, or visit earthcam.com and control the cameras on Times Square and thousands of other locations. The www.Shodan.io search engine will also supply addresses.

Tracking down cameras is not necessarily easy but can be done with time and patience. Google has a list of search strings to help you pinpoint cameras.

For newsgathering, IP camera smartphone apps offer the ability for live visual contact and coverage of events. A reporter armed with a smartphone and webcam app like SpyWebCam Pro for Android or iWebcamera for iOS can stream a live feed which can then be monitored back at base or by others in the field with mLiveCams for Android or IPCamSoft for iOS.

An editor miles from the action can switch between cameras operated by the reporters, control public and private street cameras, watch multiple views and record video segments and stills and then upload or email them onwards. They can also speak directly with each reporter using the traditional telephone feature and control the action like a live TV director.

To improve coverage, tether a wearable spy camera to the reporter's smartphone. Eventually, gadgets like Google Glass – a Borg-like headset that records live video and beams it directly to a Cloud store via the phone – may become essential kit for reporters in the field.

1.8 Secure Anonymous Blogging

Blogging is not generally illegal but people can lose their jobs through blogging and it can get you into trouble with the authorities. By its very nature, a blog will give away certain elements of your personality but not necessarily your identity if you cover your tracks.

The safest course is never to blog from home or via any personal device but to use a cybercafé or public library. You can then set up an anonymous email account and link it to an anonymous blogging account and upload from there.
Avoid locations near your usual haunts and vary them as often as possible, only choosing the busiest times. Compose the blog directly onto a portable drive and use a free program like CCleaner to clear the history on whichever device you use.

You might also add a number of simple apps to the drive, including text and photo editors and a shredder. PortableApps.com is a good source. Then shred relevant documents once the blog has been uploaded. Options include Eraser and Evidence Nuker.

If uploading your own images, be sure to remove any incriminating hidden data. Most modern cameras and smartphones add GPS data to the image's EXIF file, allowing others to pin-point your location. You can check how much data is stored in a digital photo by uploading one to exifdata.com. To clean up images before you upload then, there are numerous free tools, including ExifTool and JHead.

If you have more than one blog, use different email and blog hosts and think twice before embedding any social network links like Facebook or Twitter, or an RSS feed. Equally, never visit your blog from any device linked to you and never tweet about it under your true identity.

Generally, this will work for most eventualities but you can tighten security further by only ever accessing your blog via a hidden network. Once on Tor, you can access the email and blog sites without leaving any trace of the cybercafé's IP address. You will need to have selected both a blog site and email account that do not require JavaScript because that will also link back.

Be equally cautious in publicizing your blog. To get your message out to the most popular blog search engines use Pingomatic.com which alerts them all for you. Conversely, you might not want anyone to know about your blog, bar a select few, and will want to keep it out of the search engines. There are often options from the blog host but you can also insert a *robots.txt* into your blog that will tell the engines to stay away. To find out more, visit the Robotstxt.org website.

Another option is to avoid blog hosts and have your own website hosted anonymously in a far-off country and preferably one hostile to your own government, making court orders for disclosure meaningless.

Generally, if you want to know who owns a domain, you can look it up at www.who.is. Most registrars will give you the option of masking your WHOIS entry but, better still, anonymous name registrars will register the site in their name.

You then access all this via Tor from a cybercafé with an encrypted USB thumb drive.

However, investigators always follow the money so paying by credit card or PayPal may lead them to you. One simple option is to only pay for services with a pre-paid credit card or look for anonymous domain registrars and hosts that accept the BitCoin.

For this level of activity, a determined and sophisticated adversary will in all probability track you down eventually. It's no secret that many security services employ sophisticated algorithms to analyze a writer's style and idiosyncrasies. All they have to do then is compare the patterns with all the emails they routinely intercept and then pluck the culprit from among billions.

1.9 Keeping out the Spies

When it comes to securing your system, there are several concerns – ad networks, cybercriminals, law enforcement, intelligence agencies and corporate spies – and they all use similar techniques. Generally, they do this by so-called "social engineering", the art of enticing users to malicious websites and then tricking them into giving out confidential information or by planting malware in their system there and then or via email.

At the basic level, ad networks do this whenever users take onboard cookies. Cybercriminals make the most of news events and consumer trends to draw people to a webpage where malware will automatically plant itself in the computer, known as a "drive-by download". Malware can also be surreptitiously planted in legitimate websites to infect even the wary. These are known as "watering hole" attacks.

Within hours of the Boston marathon bombing, the spammers were sending out emails and Twitter links seemingly from CNN which sent users to sites compromised by a Blackhole Exploit Kit where many were infected by Trojans, backdoors, infostealers or rootkits. The same thing happens around most major news stories. And it's not just the gullible public who fall prey. Seasoned journalists are regularly sucked in with the apparent deaths of celebrities or by looming sex scandals.

Another growing threat is Ransomware, which locks a computer until a "fine" is paid. Infections often come via legitimate but compromised websites and advertisements where hackers have managed to insert malicious coding.
Victims suddenly find their screen frozen and a fake warning from the FBI or local law enforcement saying they have been downloading illegal content.

Even more unnerving, the perpetrators occasionally include a mug shot from the victim's own webcam. This malware is extremely hard to remove and, needless to say, once a fine has been paid the machine stays locked. Amusingly, a Chicago police department recently paid US$600 to hackers in a Ransomware sting.

If you have been the victim of the popular CoinVault Ransomware, help is at hand with the Kaspersky.com Ransomware Decryptor.

Some investigative journalist groups have reported receiving anonymous tip-offs that included either infected documents or links to malicious sites, thus allowing hackers to access their systems. It is advisable to take extreme care with anything that you receive.

Intelligence agencies and law enforcement also use malware, one example being FinSpy, which they send to people in spoof emails, allowing agents to take control of smartphones and computers, intercepting Skype calls, turning on web cameras and recording keystrokes. Researchers have found FinSpy running on 36 servers world-wide from Austria to Vietnam.

As scary as this might seem, dodgy redirects and 'drive-bys' can be pre-empted with a good anti-virus program. Equally, if you want to visit a site that may be unsafe, either because it's being run by a criminal enterprise or because law enforcement may have surreptitiously planted a tracking device, ask Google or another search engine to call up a cached version of the page. Then you are not actually visiting the site but rather a copy of it held by the search engine.

To avoid infection via email, disable HTML in your email program via the *Settings* tab. Look for and untick *Display attachments online* or tick *View message body as...plain text*.

Be aware of social media posts and emails with enticing links, many of which are often shortened so you don't know where you are heading. Short URLs can be enlarged at LongURL.org.
Never open attachments or click on links if you are unsure of their origin. If you are in the habit of reading sensitive documents, consider using a separate computer not connected to the Internet – generally known as "air-gapping" – or simply disconnect your computer from the Internet and run documents and files through an anti-virus 'sandbox'.

However, if you are under observation, it is possible for an adversary to circumvent "air-gapping" by bombarding an area or room with a Continuous Microwave Generator that effectively connects the target computer to an outside monitor. There are also reports that hackers can enter and control air-gapped computers by monitoring their heat emissions via the built-in thermal sensors.

If you feel you are being targeted and suspect something has been planted deep within your computer, you may want to consider the "nuclear option" of formatting the hard drive and reinstalling the computer's operating system. However, this only works for less sophisticated intrusion.

Some spyware can be hidden within the Bios (Basic Input/Output System) located in the computer motherboard, which is not so easy to remove. Equally, tiny hardware devices may have been planted inside the computer, or even USB leads may have been replaced that can transmit data via radio waves.

Router

It is essential to secure your home and office wireless networks from hackers. The simplest solution is to change the administrator password for the wireless router.

By default, most router manufacturers use 192.168.0.1 or 192.168.1.1 as the default LAN IP address. Type these addresses into a Web browser and your router will show up.

Hackers can then look-up the manufacturer's default password and easily break in, intercepting all the data you send and receive and seeing which devices are connected.
You should also refer to the router's handbook and switch off SSID (Service Set Identifier) broadcasting and change the default SSID name to something not easily identifiable.

It is essential to keep firmware updated and to use WPA2 encryption rather than WPA or WEP. Also switch off *Remote Access* which allows access to the router via a web browser.
USB Internet modems should be used with extreme care following a recently discovered vulnerability allowing an attacker to execute malicious code remotely by sending an SMS message to the victim, allowing access to the target's computer.

Passwords

The key to good cyber-security is a secure password that cannot be guessed at or cracked. A good password should be at least 12 characters long and should contain a mix of upper and lower case, numerals and symbols. Never use any word that you can find in a dictionary, nor names of pets or children. Do not use key dates.

On no account write down your passwords and do not store them in a dedicated password safe as the very existence of such a thing can draw attention in itself. Therefore, it must be something that you can easily remember.

As unlikely as this may seem, an ideal password would look something like this:

£iiatuata9smipoagfMbiwoaW(@_@)

On the face of it, this would appear impossible to remember. However, this password is derived from the rather memorable opening passage of the Jane Austen classic *Pride and Prejudice*, which begins like this:

It is a truth universally acknowledged that a single man in possession of a good fortune must be in want of a wife.

What we have done here is take the initial letter from each word in the first paragraph, which then looks like this:

Iiatuatasmipoagfmbiwoaw

Anybody of reasonable intelligence can easily remember this line. However, it need not be the opening passage of a book. It might be a line from a pop song or a favourite poem, or a simple phrase that you can commit to memory, but avoid anything well-known like *Mary Had a Little Lamb* or *All work and no play*.

You now need to add to this some upper case, numerals and symbols. In our chosen example we have added a "£" for its rarity value at the very beginning and then at the ninth position we have added the number 9. The words *Man* and *Woman* have been given upper case characters. Then we have added an emoticon at the end. All of this is easy to remember.

If you have a keyboard with non-universal symbols such as the UK pound (£), the Euro (€) or Yen (¥), add one of these to complicate matters further. But bear in mind that these may not be accessible when using another person's keyboard.

Hackers working to crack a password often employ a 'brute force attack' or 'exhaustive key search', but these are generally only effective against short passwords. For longer passwords, a 'dictionary attack' is often employed. The method shown here is highly effective against the most sophisticated attacks.

This, in turn, can also be used as a means of passing on a password. Once the recipient understands the principle, you just mention any book that can be found on Amazon. They look inside and read the relevant line to receive the password.

Do not use the same password for everything. However, one option is to create a basic password and then add an identifier but only use these where major security is not an issue. Also, these need not be so long.

For example, **£iiatuata9sm(@_@)Rain** might work for an Amazon account, adding the word "Rain" because the actual Amazon is a tropical rainforest and you can remember that.
However, when it comes to higher levels of security – for your email or PayPal account, etc – you need to devise unique passwords for each.

Therefore, your email account password might be based on a line from the song *Please Read the Letter* while your bank password could be derived from *Bonfire of the Vanities* by Tom Wolfe.

Remember to change your passwords regularly and ensure that your browser does not automatically remember passwords. Look in *Settings* and untick *Remember passwords for sites*.

When it comes to filling in many online forms it rarely matters if the answers are truthful or not, so there is little reason to give away valuable information that might be used elsewhere.

Aside from tax returns and passport applications, be highly cautious of using your actual date of birth (DOB). This is one of the first things an investigator looks for when tracking an individual. Equally, never give away your mother's maiden name.

Whenever signing up for a social media account, always minimize how much real information you hand over. Use a completely different DOB that you can remember and that does not tie to yourself or anyone you know. Also, it does not matter if you use this repeatedly.

Equally, it does not matter what you answer to most of these questions just so long as you can remember the answer. Therefore, when it comes to the name of your first pet or favourite food you can always use the same word each time so long as you never divulge it to anyone.

In short, whatever the security question, always stick to the same simple word for each answer. So, in answer to the questions 'What is your favourite food?' and 'The name of your first pet?' just type something largely meaningless like *Succubus* each time.

It is unlikely that anyone would ever guess this word and a hacker might waste a lot of time trying to find the real answers to the questions.

Key Loggers

Among the most dangerous forms of malware are Key Stroke Logging programs and, in extreme cases, tiny hardware versions that can be hidden inside the computer. These work by logging every keystroke and mouse movement.

Physical devices tend to be inconspicuous and may sometimes resemble a USB plug or lay hidden deep inside the machine. One option is to apply a drop of glitter nail polish to the screws at the back of the keyboard and computer unit so you can see if it has been tampered with.

If you fear a key logging program may be placed inside your device, KeyScrambler offer several solutions, including a free option, to scramble keystrokes.

Security Software

Use a combination of standalone security software with one firewall, one or two anti-virus programs, and one or two anti-spyware programs. Also consider using dedicated anti-Trojan software. Avoid running them all in 'real-time' to avoid software conflicts and, instead, regularly scan your computer with the various programs and update frequently.

You can run a quick scan of your computer for viruses, Trojans, worms, unwanted browser plugins and other malware by downloading and running HouseCall from Trend Micro which identifies and removes malevolent invaders for free. It also detects system vulnerabilities and provides links to security patches.

Recommended Free Programs

As a rule, free, open-source software is preferable to the paid-for variety because developers and others can have a good look inside for backdoors and other things that should not be there.

- Comodo Personal Firewall — free and paid-for versions of combined anti-virus and firewall programs. The firewall application uses Cloud-based data to analyze new programs and prevent attacks. It protects against viruses, Trojans, worms, hacker attacks and other threats.
- Lavasoft's Ad-Aware — free and paid-for versions. Provides core protection against Internet threats. Featuring real-time anti-

malware protection, advanced Genocode detection technology, rootkit protection and scheduler.

- Spybot Search and Destroy — free, fully functioning privacy and anti-malware software. Immunize feature blocks a range of uninvited web-borne infections before they reach your computer. Also includes Hosts File which blocks adware servers from your computer and System Startup which lets you review which apps load when you start your computer. A shredder is also included.
- AVG Anti Rootkit — removes Rootkits, a malicious program somewhere between a virus and Trojan horse which opens your computer to external attack.
- Crap Cleaner — free system-optimization tool. It removes unused and temporary files, allowing the computer to run faster and more efficiently with more hard-disk space. The application cleans traces left by Windows, Internet Explorer and third-party applications.
- MalwareBytes — finds and removes malware often missed by other programs.
- ADW Cleaner — searches for and destroys adware and PUPS (potentially unwanted programs).
- Avast Free Antivirus — full-featured software with the same antivirus and anti-spyware scanning engine used in Avast's premium products.
- AVG Anti-Virus Free Edition — probably best of the bunch when it comes to free anti-virus software.

In all these programs, be sure to check the *Settings* and turn off *automatic updating*. Manually update at regular intervals.

What's Running Now?

If your computer is running slower than usual, it may be a clue that somebody has outside control so always keep an eye on which programs are running, especially for anything new that starts up when you switch on. In Windows, open the *Task Manager* by right-clicking on the taskbar and selecting the *Processes* tab. To compare what is running on your machine against what it should typically run, see whatsrunning.net.

With Windows, you can also check to see which programs are set to start when you boot up by going to *Start/Run* and entering *msconfig* in the box. To compare your list with the most likely start up applications, see the **Start Up Applications List**.

Freeware options for viewing your start-up items and running processes include Process Explorer and CurrProcess.

Zero Emission Pads

Surveillance teams can remotely scan the electromagnetic signals from a computer monitor and reassemble the screen image. They can do this through walls and over long distances. These signals are called *compromising emanations* and in surveillance jargon the art of capturing them is known by the code word Tempest.

As a surveillance tool, this is less popular in developed countries because of the sheer amount of electrical equipment transmitting in the 100KHz - 2MHz range and because people have moved away from CRT monitors to LCD.

You can prevent people looking in by using a Zero Emission Pad – a software program which defuses the compromising rays.

Cleaning Up

The Heidi Eraser is freeware that allows you to completely remove sensitive data from a Windows hard drive by overwriting it several times with carefully selected patterns. The *Erase Secure Move* feature erases all traces after you move files from one place to another. Eraser can also be set to erase the Windows *pagefile* on *shutdown/restart* and it has the option of being added to your context menu, so when you right-click a file you can select *Erase*.

Erasing History

Almost every piece of software wants to store information about you and what you like to do. Internet browsers keep a record of your browsing history and downloads. PDF readers store a history of the files you've read. MS Office records recently opened documents and words in the documents. Media players store details of recently played files.

To erase your tracks in one go consider dedicated cleaning software like CCleaner. When choosing software, select one that gives you the option to specify the number of times data is overwritten. A minimum of three 'passes' is recommended.

Apple iOS

Many people believe Macs are safer but they are just as susceptible to attack as any other operating system. There tends to be less malware aimed at iOS because it is not as popular as Windows, which is where most cybercriminals concentrate their activity. The same is true of the iPhone over the Android. According to security experts Symantec.com, one percent of Mac users were compromised in 2012 by the Flashback attack which allowed for remote access. Curiously, Mac users are less likely to invest in anti-virus software. However, the NSA is reported to have paid special attention to Apple products, particularly the iPhone, so it should not be used in highly-sensitive situations.

Windows OS

Windows is no longer supporting its XP operating system which means there will never be another security update. It is now more vulnerable than ever. For those addicted to Windows, keep abreast of newer versions.

Windows, because it is designed for the mass market, is an inherently insecure operating system that runs a lot of unnecessary services that can put your computer at risk. As a result, it is best to disable any unused services. Doing so will also help increase the speed of your computer.

- First, open the *Computer Management* window
- Right-click *My Computer*
- Click *Manage*
- Expand *Services and Applications*
- Select *Services/Standard* tab

If any service status shows *Started*, and you are not using it, click *Actions* and then the *Stop* button. If you are unsure, read the item *Description*. If still in doubt, leave as is. To change from *Automatic* to *Manual*, etc, click *Action*, *Properties*, *General*. Then click on *Apply* and *OK* when you have finished.

- Application Management — set to Manual.
- Automatic Updates — for downloading and installing Windows updates. It is best to *Disable* and update manually.
- ClipBook — Disable
- COM+ Event System — Disable if you are not programming in Visual Studio .NET. If you are programming in VS .NET set to Manual.
- COM+ System Application — Disable if you are not programming in Visual Studio .NET. If you are programming in VS .NET set to Manual.

- Computer Browser — Disable. This lists all computers on a network and gives information to other computers on the same network. This service is unnecessary and, even while *Disabled*, you can still browse the network.
- Distributed Link Tracking Client — Disable if you are not on a network. This is only applicable when you use the NTFS file system. If you don't, you can switch off this service.
- Error Reporting Service — Disable. This reports system errors to Microsoft.
- Fax Service — Disable if you do not use the internal fax machine.
- Help and Support — set to Manual.
- Human Interface Device Access — Disable.
- IPSEC Services — Disable if you are not using remote connection to a company network.
- Messenger — Disable. This service has nothing to do with Live Messenger.
- Net Meeting Remote Desktop Sharing — Disable. This service opens your computer to inspection and control by others computers as a remote desktop.
- Network DDE — Disable.
- Performance Logs and Alerts — Disable.
- Protected Storage — Disable. This service stores passwords which can be easily retrieved.
- Remote Access Auto Connection Manager — Disable.
- Remote Desktop Help Session Manager — Disable.
- Remote Registry — Disable. This service allows external users to make changes to your registry keys.
- Removable Storage — set to Manual.
- Routing and Remote Access — Disable.
- Security Center — Disable. This service monitors the functioning of your system security (Windows updates, firewall and virus scan).
- Server — Disable if you are not on a network.
- System Event Notification — Disable.

- System Restore Service — Disable. This service allows Windows to restore your system to an earlier date and opens your computer to inspection from different points in the past.
- Themes — Disable.
- Windows Image Acquisition (WIA) — Disable. This service transfers images from your camera/web cam or scanner.
- Wireless Zero Configuration — Disable if you are not using a wireless connection.

Windows Security Center
Window's own built-in Security Center and Firewall are woefully ineffective and should be *Disabled* via the Control Panel and replaced with a third party firewall instead.

Pagefile/Swapfile

By default, Windows creates a file on your hard drive (*pagefile.sys*) which it uses as additional computer memory. Most modern computers, those with over 1GB of RAM, don't need this so it should be *Disabled*. Go to *Control Panel*, *System*, *Advanced* tab, then select the *Settings* button under the *Performance* heading, *Advanced* tab, *Virtual Memory*, *Change*, select *No Paging File*, click *Set*, then *OK*.

Hibernation
Windows Hibernation Mode needs to be *Disabled* as it saves current data to your hard drive in plaintext which can then be retrieved. Go *Control Panel*, *Power Options*, *Hibernate* tab, then uncheck *Enable Hibernation*.

Alternative Software
Microsoft's own software leaks like a sieve and is best replaced with the open source variety. Avoid using Office, Outlook, Internet Explorer, and Windows Media Player as they collaborate with each other.

- Use **Open Office Suite** instead of MS Office (Word, Excel, etc). Always disable *auto-save* in the program options.
- Use **VLC Media Player** instead of Windows Media Player.
- Use **Foxit PDF Reader** instead of Adobe Acrobat Reader. Be sure to tick *Enable Safe Reading Mode*. And untick *Restore Last View Setting when Reopening*.

Part 2 - Deep Search

Introduction

When it comes down to it, there is no great mystery to the Deep Web. It's a big place, for sure, but there are notable landmarks to help you find your way around. This 'hidden' Internet may be made up of squillions of petabytes of data stored around the planet but very little is truly hidden. You just need to know where to look.

For the everyday things, Google and the conventional search engines do a good job. But detailed information is not always easy to find, especially when the engines throw up thousands of pages of results.

Most people rarely venture beyond the first page or two and after 14 minutes of fruitless looking even the most determined usually give up.

Understanding how to interrogate any search engine will certainly help. But knowing where to look is often more important.

The regular search engines only index a tiny fraction of the data stored on the Internet. They do this by extracting the 'visible' data on websites. This is then searchable with keywords.

The information held on the Deep Web is largely contained inside databases and archives and this content is not indexed by the conventional engines because they are rarely programmed to enter these data stores.

As such, this so-called "Deep Web" information can only be found by interrogating the database or archive directly through their own search facilities. The archives themselves can usually be found by asking a conventional Surface search engine to find them for you.

For example, suppose a Boeing 767 crashes and you want to look for similar incidents. You would begin your search in the conventional way with Google. But rather than asking Google to find the actual information itself, ask it to find a database dealing with air accidents, such as PlaneCrashInfo.com.

The data held within this site is, therefore, Deep Web because it will not have been indexed by the Surface search engines so they won't know what is inside. But, once at the database, you can directly enter the make and model of the aircraft, along with a daterange, and pull up every accident report for every incident globally, along with all the probable causes. Trying to do this by interrogating a Surface search engine alone would take more time than most people are ever likely to devote.

The same thing works for historical documents and quotations. For example, you may come across the line "I am the most unhappy man. I have unwittingly ruined my country" and want to pin it down.

Google will certainly provide the apparent quote by Woodrow Wilson – *"I am the most unhappy man. I have unwittingly ruined my country. A great industrial nation is now controlled by its system of credit. We are no longer a government by free opinion, no longer a government by conviction and the vote of the majority, but a government by the opinion and duress of a small group of dominant men"*.

But what you see is not necessarily the actual quotation and you will also see endless examples of people regurgitating the line without pinning it down to a time and a place or to a specific document. You will also see a lot of debate as to its validity because most people do not know how to search effectively. But, by knowing that Woodrow Wilson said this, Google can find the right archive, taking you to woodrowwilson.org where you can quickly track part of the line down to a 1912 campaign speech and find the remainder in the full-text version of Wilson's book *The New Freedom* published in 1913, the year he signed the Federal Reserve into existence. You could spend all day on Google and achieve nothing, as opposed to 20 minutes of reading in the right archive.

So it is not that difficult. You just need to know where to look and, of course, how to phrase the right question.
It would be difficult for this book to list every possible archive and database and all the other portals within the Deep Web, but below you will find some of the most useful. For the rest, ask a conventional search engine.

2.1 How to Search

Searching on the Deep Web is just like searching on the Surface Web. You need to know where to look, how to phrase your question and how to refine the search; so it helps to understand the main types of search service out there and how they work.

As obvious as it might seem, web searching is a matter of selecting the right words and devising a strategy to find what you are looking for. Unfortunately, not all search engines use the same rules but it helps to understand the basic way most engines work. Google, for example, uses Boolean logic, as do many of the popular engines. The examples below will work for most of them.

Phrase Search — by putting double quotes (" ") around a set of words, a Boolean engine knows to consider the exact words in that exact order. An example might be "fish and chips" which will show all documents containing that same phrase (12 million results), rather than all documents containing the word *fish* and all documents with the word *chips* (40 million results). Engines tend to ignore the word *and* when lower-case because it is too common to log. You can also use double quotes to track down documents that you know contains a specific phrase, such as "Under the Federal Reserve Act panics are scientifically created". By wrapping this sentence in quotes, Google and other Boolean engines will find around 20,000 documents containing a quote from 1929 by adventurer and Congressman Charles Lindbergh, whose baby son was famously kidnapped. This is effectively half the results if you had typed the sentence without the quotes. This also works for names. The query "George Bush" will throw up over 70 million results, but take the quotes away and you have more than 225 million to choose from. Do note that some search engines have a maximum limit of ten words so, if you are highlighting a particular quotation, select just ten of those words. Google recently increased its count to 32 words.

Excluding Words — a minus sign (-) immediately before a word tells the engine that you do not want pages containing this particular word. If you want to know more about Charles Lindbergh but want to remove all references to the kidnapping of his baby son in 1932, you would type "Charles Lindbergh" -kidnapping. This will reduce the results by about 200,000. Some engines prefer the word NOT in place of the minus sign, such as "Airedale Terrier" NOT breeders (note Google prefers the – sign, while AltaVista is happy with either).

Wildcard — the asterisk symbol (*) tells the engine to treat the asterisk as a missing word and to come up with the best matches. Typing Google * will call up a list of all of Google's services, from Google Translate through to Google Sky. The asterisk is also handy when looking for a word that has variants, like *smoking* but you would also like to see references to *smokers*, *smoke* and *smoked*. Try *smok**.

Using OR — by using the word OR in capital letters, engines can serve up a range of variables. To find a library or archive devoted to Lindbergh you would type "Charles Lindbergh" library OR archive and thereby widen your scope. Some engines prefer not to use OR but use the | symbol instead.

Using AND — another seemingly obvious one but something often neglected in web searches. By adding the word AND (or with some engines the + symbol) to a search phrase, specific elements are added to the search. Typing "Charles Lindbergh" AND economy will bring up results linking him with the economy. However, if we wanted to exclude results about fuel economy, we would add a minus sign: "Charles Lindbergh" AND economy -fuel.

Connections — use the underscore symbol (_) when looking for pairs of words that are directly connected, for example quick_start.

Search within a website — Boolean engines can be asked to search within a specific website for their results. Typing Afghanistan site:www.time.com will produce a breakdown of all references to Afghanistan in Time Magazine.

Domain Search — domains are broken down by country, such as *.af* for Afghanistan and *co.uk* for the United Kingdom, and by type of organization such as *.org* for non-profit making organization or *.edu* for education in the United States. Typing "hamid karzai" site:af will bring up everything listed on sites with an Afghan domain referencing the President. Typing Afghanistan site:gov will return results only from a US *.gov* domain.

Search by Document Type — often detailed information, especially studies and reports, can be found by seeking out particular document types. A request for Afghanistan filetype:PDF will offer only PDF files. Typing Afghanistan filetype:ppt will give results for PowerPoint Presentations, and *xls* for spreadsheets. Be alert that certain files types – MS Word, Excel and PDF especially – may contain viruses and should be opened with caution. Where possible, use the *View as HTML* option.

Search Titles — many engines give you the option to search for keywords in the title of documents. intitle:Afghanistan AND landmines will take you to all documents but these will also include news reports. Reduce this by typing intitle:afghanistan AND landmines filetype:ppt and you will be offered only PPP documents that contain these words in the title. Also be aware that different ways of spelling will influence the results, so you might want to type intitle:Afghanistan AND landmines OR "land mines". Using *allintitle* restricts results to documents containing all the keywords. For example allintitle:afghanistan drugs warlords.

Synonym Search — by inserting a tilde (~) in front of a word, most engines will search for the word and its synonyms. A search including the words *computer ~security* will also produce results covering encryption, malware, firewall, etc.

Search in URLs — website addresses (URLs) often contain clues to their subject matter, so you can seek out websites devoted to particular issues. For example, inurl:Airedale will offer websites purely devoted to the King of Terriers.

Related Site Search — using *related:* will bring up a short list of sites either similar to or in some way related or linked to a particular website, for example related:www.airedale.com.

Reverse Link Searching — websites and databases that you find particularly useful are often linked to by other equally interesting sites that you might also want to explore. To find out which sites link to the Internet Movie Database, for example, type link:www.imdb.com.

Cache Search — to search for sites and pages that no longer exist, typing cache:www.airedale.com will show the last stored version of that page. This is also particularly useful when researching sensitive subjects and not wanting to visit the actual website itself in case of "drive-by downloads" and the like.

Lucky Search — adding certain types of words to a search can produce interesting results, especially when you are looking for documents that may have been inadvertently posted online. These include "not for distribution", "company proprietary", "confidential", "secret", etc. Typing filetype:xls site:za confidential will produce several hundred pages of confidential business information from South Africa.

Number Search — to find numbers within a given range of things like prices, measurements, temperatures, separate numbers with two periods, like this shoes $30..$90.

Search by Date — not easy as most engines do not have a facility to date search, although Google does via the *Search Tools* tab. However, if dates do show up, they refer to the last time a particular page was indexed rather than created or modified. The ability to search by date is helpful as it allows you to weed out older documents and select the latest versions or search for news stories around a particular time. You can type in *daterange:* and then the date but most engines operate on Julian Time, a scientific system of time measurement, so you will need a Julian Time converter. The date 7 July 2000, for example, appears as 2451733.06531. To make matters worse, decimal points confuse most engines, so you have to drop the point and the last five digits. If we want to pin down the Afghan president to a particular time-frame, say the first two days of April 2012, we would input daterange:2456019-2456020 Hamid Karzai (or Hamid Karzai daterange:2456019-2456020) and now we have just 13,000 results to choose from and a better chance of refining the search further. (Additionally, it may help on some engines to drop the quotes around phrases when using *daterange*.) However, while this works for contemporary characters, it is less successful with historical ones. If we want to find out what Charles Lindbergh was up to between 20 May 1927 and 20 June that year, we would type "Charles Lindbergh" daterange:2425021-2425052. While this does narrow down the search, it is far from satisfactory as it includes many dates outside that range.

The Exalead search engine has a date search facility that allows you to search *before* and *after* dates, i.e. Mohammed Karzai before:2004/05/21 and Mohammed Karzai after:2004/05/21.

2.2 Search Engines

Search engines work by storing key information from the webpages that they retrieve using an automated web browser known as a Crawler. This information is extracted from the site's title page, content, headings and meta tags. Results are generally presented in list form and can cover webpages, images and some file types. A few engines also mine data inside databases but coverage is a long way from comprehensive.

Some search engines like Google store all or part of the source page (known as a cache). Others, like AltaVista, store every word of every page they find. When a user enters a query into a search engine, the engine examines its index and provides a listing of best-matching webpages, usually with a short summary containing the document's title and sometimes some of the text. The engine looks for words or phrases exactly as entered.

Most search engines rank their results to provide the "best" results first. How a search engine decides which are the best pages tends to vary.

Most search engines are in it for the money and some charge advertisers to have their listings ranked higher. Those which don't charge make money by placing search-related ads alongside the regular search results and get paid whenever someone clicks on an ad.

Google Alternatives — Google, along with most search engines, stores detailed information about your interests. Each year, the FBI compels these companies to hand over the personal details of hundreds of users without presenting a court order. There are, however, alternative engines that do not store information on you in the first place:

- IxQuick
- Startpage
- DuckDuckGo
- Secret Search Labs

Deep Web Search — no single engine can search the entire Deep Web and no single directory can cover it all, but these go some way:
- InfoMine — built by librarians at the University of California, California State University, the University of Detroit-Mercy, and Wake Forest University.
- Librarians' Internet Index — search engine listing sites deemed trustworthy by librarians.
- SurfWax — practical tools for dynamic search and navigation.
- BUBL — catalogue of Internet resources.
- Pinakes Subject Launch Pad — academic research portal.
- Search.com — dozens of topic-based databases from CNet.
- OAIster Database — millions of digital resources from thousands of contributors.

Metasearch Engines
A good way to perform a detailed search is to employ a metasearch engine to search multiple search engines simultaneously. These include:
- DogPile
- Mamma
- Kartoo

Database Search — there are specialized search engines for finding databases. Arguably the best of the bunch is CompletePlanet which scours over 70,000 searchable databases and specialty search engines. Other notables include:
- Search.com — seeks out databases and allows you to search multiples engines with a single query.
- TheInfo.com — search specific engines and databases.

- Beaucoup.com— one of the first specialized search engine guides, listing over 2,500 selected engines, directories and indices.
- FinderSeeker — breaks searches down by country and even cities.
- Fossick — covers over 3,000 specialized search engines and databases.

Databases and Gateways
- Repositories of Primary Sources — direct links to over 5,000 archives, databases and websites globally.
- WWW Virtual Library — first catalogue of the web, started by Tim Berners-Lee in 1991. Run by a loose confederation of volunteers.
- Librarians' Internet Index — compiled by librarians offering a searchable, human-reviewed gateway to quality sites in the Surface and Deep Webs.
- Digital Librarian — a librarian's choice for the best of the web's databases and research resources.
- GPO — US Government Printing Office, access to multiple databases including records, hearings, reports, manuals, court opinions, etc.
- Library of Congress Catalogs — gateway to a vast collection of academic institutions, universities, libraries, and miscellaneous databases.
- CIA Electronic Reading Room — search for declassified CIA documents.
- Project Vote Smart — database of US government officials and candidates.
- USPTO — patient full-text and image database.
- US Census Bureau International Database — demographics, world population data, etc.
- WebLens — portal to academic and scholarly research papers and thousands of useful Internet research tools.

- DOAJ — Directory of Open Access Journals, free full-text scientific and scholarly journals, covering numerous subjects and languages.
- Geniusfind — directory of thousands of search engines, databases and archives organized into categories and subcategories.
- Ask Eric — education resources information center.

Open Directories — assembled by human beings who use editorial judgment to make their selections and not by Crawlers running algorithms. A web directory is not a search engine and does not display lists of webpages based on keywords but divides the web into categories.

The categorization is usually based on the whole website rather than one page or a set of keywords. Most directories are general in scope and list websites across a wide range of subjects, regions and languages. But some niche directories focus on countries, languages, industries, products, etc.

Popular directories include the Yahoo! Directory and the very comprehensive Open Directory Project.

User-Edited Directories — are compiled, as the name suggests, by users who are generally experts in their field and who wish to share favorite sites and improve search results. These include IllumiRate and JoeAnt.

2.3 Search Sources

People Search

There are a range of specialty search tools for tracking down individuals. Most concentrate on the US but these will often pull up people from elsewhere on the planet, depending where they are listed.

- Pipl.com — the best place to begin a search. Pipl casts a very wide net, searching within social networks, websites, blogs, magazines and newspapers, phone and public records, background checks, criminal records and even within classified advertisements. Works well internationally.
- NameChk.com — once you have a person's social media username you can look for other instances of its use elsewhere on the Internet.
- WebMii.com — find online public information. Good for finding physical and email address, plus phone numbers.
- Yasni.co.uk UK — free UK people search.
- Yoname.com — good, across-the-board people search internationally.
- LinkedIn.com — business-orientated social networking service, helpful for verifying individuals and for finding further leads.
- Spokeo.com — primarily a US-based search facility with email and username search and reverse address and telephone look-up. Was once free, now charging for searches.
- Abika.com — again, primarily US but very detailed search including criminal records by state, county and Federal, also global civil and criminal search, tax records, mortgages, evictions, background checks, personality profiles, traffic violations, vehicle history; plus image, audio and video search.
- Zabasearch.com — also US but claims to offer three-times more residential listings than the White Pages. Also offers reverse phone lookup.

- **Public Records** http://publicrecords.onlinesearches.com/— a gateway to public records across the US.
- **Find County Records** http://www.findcountyrecords.com/— directory of US county public records.
- Jail Base — free and paid-for service offering jail inmate searches across the US.
- 123people.com — free international people search including social network usernames.
- 192.com — excellent paid-for people and business search in the United Kingdom.
- Find My Past — search family records from Britain, Ireland, Australasia and the US. Subscription service.
- **UK National Archives** http://www.nationalarchives.gov.uk — covers births, death and marriages, military records, employment, Census, etc.
- Numberway — links to international White and Yellow page phone books.
- FoneFinder — free, international reverse telephone number lookup.
- CEOEmail**.com** — find the personal email addresses of CEOs of UK companies.
- Creepy http://ilektrojohn.github.io/creepy — aptly-named free geolocation open-source intelligence (OSInt) tool that allows for target tracking using Twitter, Flickr and Instagram posts. Enter a Twitter user-name and see all the locations that the user has posted from, together with their Tweets and photo captions. Refine searches to location, time or date, and export to Google Maps for in-depth analysis.
- GeoSocialFootprint**.com** — track peoples' haunts and locations using a combination of social media postings, GPS-enabled tweets, social check-ins, geocoding and profile harvesting.

Social Network Search

- Topsy.com — excellent service which allows you to search for Twitter users across Twitter and other media, viewing their entire tweet timelines and references to them, etc. Also allows for date and language search.
- Monitter.com — real-time Twitter search tool that allows you to monitor Twitter for mentions of any words or phrases, people, places or usernames, and from specific locations.
- Facebook Directory — search people listed publicly on Facebook.
- SocialMention.com — search trends across social networks and receive email alerts – covers people and celebrities, products, brands and companies, news events, etc.
- Identify — Firefox plugin creates a profile of individuals' social media identities from any page.

Paid-for Search Services
- Cision.com — comprehensive people watching service with real-time monitoring and analysis reports covering blogs, micro-blogs, social networks, forums, video and image-sharing sites, news sources, print and broadcast media. Track the impact of a story, identify key developments, trace individuals across the web.
- Sysomos.com — business intelligence for social media, provides instant access to all social media conversations from blogs, social networks and micro-blogging services to forums, video sites and media sources.

Business Search
- **FT Search** http://search.ft.com — search the Financial Times' archives, company profiles and business news with over 10 million full-text articles from 2,000 different European, Asian and American business sources. US$10 per month.
- TechRepublic.com — the web's largest library of free technical IT white papers, webcasts and case studies. Covering data

management, IT management, networking, communications, enterprise applications, storage, security, etc.

- GuideStar.org — information on 640,000 non-profit organizations including recent tax returns.
- FoundationCenter.org — providing information on over 70,000 foundations, including grants. Look up organizations, identify funding sources, check statistics.
- **Gb.**Kompass.com — search products, services and companies.

Economic Search

- EconoMagic.com — links to over 400,000 data files with charts and excel files for each. Broad coverage including economic forecasts, indicators, reports, etc.
- Free Lunch www.economy.com/freelunch/default.asp — free economic, demographic and financial data.
- eFinancialBot — global search engine for financial resources.

Science and Engineering Search

- Scirus.com — said to be the most comprehensive scientific research tool on the web. With over 545 million scientific items indexed, search for journal content and scientists' homepages, courseware, pre-print server material, patents and institutional repository and website information.
- TechXtra.ac.uk — find articles, websites, books, industry news, job announcements, e-journals, e-prints, technical reports, research, thesis and dissertations.
- E-Print Network www.osti.gov/eprints/— integrated network of electronic, scientific and technical information created by scientists and research engineers. All full-text searchable. Gateway to over 35,000 websites and databases worldwide, containing over 5.5 million e-prints in basic and applied sciences, primarily in physics but also chemistry, biology and life sciences,

materials science, nuclear sciences and engineering, energy research, computer and information technologies.

- ScienceResearch.com — comprehensive public **SCIENCE** and technology research portal, searching over 300 collections globally.
- Science.gov — search over 55 databases and over 2,100 selected websites from 13 Federal agencies, offering 200 million pages of US government science information including research and development results.
- WorldWideScience.**org**— search portal to international science databases in multiple languages.
- CiteSeer — database of technical and scientific literature sponsored by the School of Information Sciences and Technology at Penn State University.
- NTIS.gov — National Technical Information Service offers a keyword-searchable database of unclassified government-sponsored technical and scientific reports. Reports are downloadable and generally cost under $20.

Medical Search
- MedBioWorld.com — resource portal for professional medical and biotechnology information.
- UCLA Health www.mednet.ucla.edu/ — information resources for physicians and staff.
- PubMed www.ncbi.nlm.nih.gov/pubmed/— comprises more than 22 million citations for biomedical literature from MedLine, life science journals and online books.
- DrugBank.ca — vast database of medicinal drugs.

Art Search
- Musee du Louvre www.louvre.fr— find works at the Louvre, the Department of Prints and Drawings, and works in French museums.

- Guggenheim.org — searchable database of selected artworks from the Guggenheim's permanent collection. The site contains more than 1,100 artworks by over 450 artists. Also includes works from the Peggy Guggenheim Collection Venice, and the Guggenheim Museum Bilbao.
- National Portrait Gallery http://npgportraits.si.edu— more than 100,000 portrait records from the Catalog of American Portraits, a survey of American portraits in public and private collections across the US and abroad. National Portrait Gallery collections are included in this database.
- Smithsonian National Portrait Gallery http://npgportraits.si.edu/code/emuseum.asp— find portraits for more than 80,000 people in this database.
- Your Paintings www.bbc.co.uk/arts/yourpaintings/— the entire UK national collection of oil paintings and the stories behind them. The digital archive is made up of paintings from thousands of museums and other public institutions around Britain.

Image and Media Search
- Google Image Search — search over 880 million image files. Searches for keywords within the image filename, captions and accompanying text.
- TinEye.com — reverse image search. Enter an image and see where it exists on the web.
- Free-Ocr.com — extracts text from images which can then be run through Google Translate or other mapping resources.
- FindExif.com — reveal Exif data from images.
- FotoForensics.com — check to see if an image has been altered.
- InternetArchive.org — superb digital library offering free access to books, movies, music and sound recordings, as well as 271 billion archived webpages. Includes the WayBack Machine http://archive.org/web/web.php for a snapshot of websites from different points in their past.

- PicSearch.com — image search service with more than 3,000,000,000 pictures.
- Yale University Library http://digitalcollections.library.yale.edu/— access over 500,000 digital images.
- Harvard University Library http://digitalcollections.harvard.edu/— vast historical image collection.
- NYPL Digital Gallery http://digitalgallery.nypl.org/nypldigital/index.cfm— open access to over 800,000 images digitized from the New York Public Library's vast collections, including illuminated manuscripts, historical maps, vintage posters, rare prints and photographs.
- Sonic http://www.loc.gov/rr/record/Sonicintro.html— Library of Congress Recorded Sound Collection contains 2.5 million audio recordings on a variety of formats representing the history of sound recording from late 19th century cylinders and discs to digital files, include radio broadcasts and spoken word, as well as vocal and instrumental music.
- BeeMP3.com — search engine for locating mp3 audio files with over 800,000 in the database.
- blinkx.com — vast video search engine.
- MetaTube.com — browse 100 of the most popular video sharing sites simultaneously.

Appendix

3.1 Cloud Storage – the Problems

US intelligence agencies can legally access – without the need for a warrant – any data stored in a US-owned Cloud service following a recent amendment to the Foreign Intelligence Surveillance Act.

This effectively gives them *carte blanche* to monitor journalists, politicians, activists and others world-wide. While US citizens are excused this intrusion thanks to the Fourth Amendment, Washington can access the personal data of any non-US citizen outside of the US if it is stored in a Cloud service run by a US company.

Under the existing law – introduced in 2008 to retroactively legalize "warrantless wiretapping" – US agencies legally monitor phone calls and emails in and out of the country. Now "remote computing services" have been added to the list of targets which could literally mean anything stored on a computer other than your own.

The NSA and FBI tap directly into the Cloud servers of at least nine leading US Internet companies, including Google, Facebook and Microsoft, allowing agents to track foreign and domestic targets. Under the NSA's PRISM program, people, organizations and even countries that store data this way are open to deep surveillance by algorithms tasked with safeguarding national security. PRISM allows for real-time monitoring of email, Skype calls, live chats and file transfers and is said to be "the most prolific contributor to the President's Daily Brief".

Remarkably, this means the US can also access any British government documents stored online including ministerial files, local authority records, and public sector data.

At least four US companies are involved in the UK government's G-Cloud project. Eventually, it is planned that the G-Cloud will hold the bulk of State data in addition to that of schools, charities, the BBC and police, even the Bank of England. Britain wants to see even greater use of Cloud storage across all sectors in what it describes as a robust "public cloud first policy".

Cloud storage is increasingly popular world-wide with around one-third of businesses in the West and an unknown number of private users employing some form of remote storage from US-based companies like Apple, Amazon and Google.

The Cloud, however, should be considered a major cause for concern in its own right. There is debate as to who legally owns what if it is stored or edited in the Cloud and you can't even bequest your online music collection to a loved one when you die. Apple routinely scans emails in its iCloud for contentious words or phrases, such as "barely legal teen" and refuses to pass them on to the recipient.

NSA aside, hackers can more easily access data en-route to the Cloud than they can on a local area network, and the Cloud administrators might one day be compromised. The companies themselves may go bust or be taken over. They might suffer some catastrophic event or decide to amended their terms and conditions.

"If businesses or governments think they might be spied on," says Neelie Kroes, vice president of the European Commission, "they will have less reason to trust the Cloud, and it will be Cloud providers who ultimately miss out. Why would you pay someone else to hold your commercial or other secrets, if you suspect or know they are being shared against your wishes?"

3.2 The BitCoin

Transferring money without leaving a trace is far from easy. However, the Deep Web's own currency the BitCoin may provide the solution. Not just for paying off hit men or buying industrial quantities of horse tranquillizer, the BitCoin can be used for all sorts of online transactions from ordering flowers to buying karaoke equipment.

This is electronic money, a crypto-currency that does away with the need for banks by combining a limited quantity digital currency with state of the art cryptographic security and a peer-to-peer network. All transactions are irreversible. It is also free, unlike Visa or PayPal.

How does it work? It's a little complex but in essence BitCoin is open-source software invented by the pseudonymous **Satoshi Nakamoto** that logs all transactions on the network and records them on Blockchain.info. The first BitCoins were issued on January 3, 1998.

The number of BitCoins is limited by the design of the network. There will never be more than 21 million BitCoins which means they are likely to increase in value unlike conventional currencies.

The value of a BitCoin is determined by the automated online markets which match buyers and their bid prices with sellers and their asking prices.

BitCoin transactions are anonymous and identified only by their BitCoin address, which need not link to any existing conventional account. However, when making payments to an exchange or bank account, the BitCoin address may link back to you – opening all your digital transactions to scrutiny. In which case, open a number of BitCoin addresses and move the money around them first. You can have as many BitCoin addresses as you wish.

Because there is no single issuing authority, there is no single point of failure which, in today's financial climate, can only be a bonus. If your bank goes under you may lose your money but it's unlikely that the Internet will collapse any time soon and take down the BitCoin network (although there are some who fear it might).

Payments are sent with one click like email and are just as swift. Accounts cannot be frozen and nobody need know what you are buying. BitCoin recognizes no national boundaries nor has limitations on where money can be sent.
You can use BitCoins online for millions of items and even make donations to charities. You can also make purchases at physical shops and restaurants that accept them. See the BitCoin trade wiki for a list of online and real world businesses.

BitCoins can be purchased in the same way that you buy any currency. You can ask your bank to buy them for you (but not many banks are up to speed on BitCoins yet) or pay via Visa or Western Union, etc. They can also be bought and sold with a **mobile app.**

The simplest solution is to visit the Blockchain.ino website and start a new 'wallet'. From there you can transfer money from most bank accounts to the wallet by following the on-screen instructions.

BitCoins are also infinitely divisible. You can send someone 0.00000001 of a BitCoin for a very small item or any amount you hold.

Some people see them as a good investment. Back in December 2010, one BitCoin was worth about US$0.22. Today, it is trading at over US$500. It recently climbed to astronomical levels but has settled down

However, with all other financial transactions globally passing through US-owned computers and therefore under constant observation by the agencies, the BitCoin is likely to become a target for increased government attention.

Also see the informative visual at http://www.fxcm.com/bitcoin/.

3.3 Other Hidden Networks

Usenet Newsgroups — rich source for all manner of media files that other people have posted that can be downloaded without drawing attention. They are also ideal for surreptitious communications.

Newsgroups are rather like an email system or bulletin board where anybody can post on any subject and anybody else can read those messages and download attachments. You need special Newsreader software and a low-cost subscription to the network. It can be installed on any operating system.

Usenet – which remarkably has been around since 1980 – has been largely ignored by Internet users probably because it does not have the same glitzy appeal of the World Wide Web but rather resembles an endless list of discussion topics, which is precisely what you do see.

During the 1991 coup attempt in Russia to oust President Gorbachev, activists used Newsgroups to get news in and out of the country and to communicate secretly among themselves.

Usenet is Deep Web and it is secure if you take the right precautions. It can defeat Deep Packet Inspection because it prevents the ISP from seeing inside the data by using secure 256-bit SSL encryption.

Although your ISP can tell if you are accessing Usenet, once you pass beyond the curtain, everything you do there is hidden from inspection.
There are Newsgroups devoted to every conceivable subject from *alt.fan.jackie-chan* and *alt.aviation.jobs* to *alt.binaries.sounds.mp3.world-music.*

The most popular Usenet Newsreader software is Free Agent, available in both free and paid-for versions. A network subscription costs US$4.99 per month upwards and gives access to an enormous store of digital material going back years, offering a better option than torrents for downloading without drawing attention. To see what is available, visit the search engine at binsearch.info.

A popular provider is Giganews http://www.giganews.com/with bundled Mimo newsreader and add-ons, including the useful and speedy Vypr Virtual Private Network (VPN) which further masks you on Usenet and allows you to browse the Surface Web with a high degree on anonymity by pretending to be in any one of several countries.

Downloading from Usenet is secure, in that nobody can see what you are doing. Uploading sensitive material is slightly more risky and requires extra layers of security. For this, you will need to implement the following steps:

- Do not use credit cards or PayPal when signing up with a Usenet provider. Many will accept the BitCoin or pre-paid credit cards, leaving you free to write what you like in the contact details.
- Add a free VPN or one that accepts BitCoins to mask your activities from your ISP.
- Sign up using Tor or the VPN so they cannot see where you are coming from (but do not combine Tor and Usenet access as this places strain on the Tor network).
- Avoid signing up with any companies based in the United States.
- Install the Newsreader and VPN onto a USB thumb drive and access them from there.
- Split and reassemble large files using HJSplit and upload the various parts to different groups. Do not give names that identify them. Items can also be placed inside RAR or 7z files and encrypted.

Rather like placing a cryptic notice in *The Times*, messages can be sent and received by placing them inside any group you like, preferably the dullest possible. By placing your message in the group *alt.emircpih.pets.porcupines* and giving it a header that no one will want to open such as *Spam-Buster Pro*, you will have placed a needle inside the vastest of all possible haystacks that nobody without prior knowledge will ever be able to find.

Freenet — free software which lets you anonymously share files, browse and publish Freenet websites. You can also do many of the usual things like chat on forums and post on boards. Freenet encrypts everything and routes it through other nodes to make it extremely difficult to determine who is requesting the information and what its content is. However, users are obliged to contribute to the network by giving bandwidth and a portion of their hard drive for storing files. Freenet Gateway <!> http://2vlqpcqpjlhmd5r2.onion/

i2P — a little similar to Tor (in that it routes traffic through other peers and is encrypted end-to-end), i2P is an 'anonymizing network' using several layers of encryption, gives access to email services, peer-to-peer, IRC chat, and other things.

Hyperboria**.net** — global, decentralized network offering secure communications and an "alternative to the Internet".

Even Deeper

Initially, investigators will be looking in the most obvious places, so communicate somewhere odd. An idea place is within the Usenet Newsgroups where messages and attachments can easily be hidden within innocuous-sounding groups.

A recent Snowden revelation shows that the NSA and GCHQ have been infiltrating the realm of the Massively Multiplayer Online Role-Playing Games (MMORPG) in their attempts to track terrorists and money-launderers.

However, it is unlikely that these agencies are monitoring every single conversation in Planet Arkadia or My Little Pony World.

With World of War Craft (WoW) drawing over 12 million participants and Second Life refusing to disclose any information about its residents, there are sizable crowds to hide amongst. At WoW, you can voice chat and PM as an Elf to an Orc; and few intelligence operatives are going to be watching you then.

Criminals and worse discovered these virtual worlds long ago and use them to launder money and make payments. Today, the virtual currencies of these two virtual worlds are so huge as to be listed on the real world currency markets. Who is to say you didn't mine a ton of virtual gold in the mythical land of Azeroth?

*
Share the Knowledge
If you found this book helpful, please recommend Deep Web for Journalists to a fellow journalist.

www.alanpearce.com
books@alanpearce.com

Useful Links

Avast - https://www.avast.com
Hotspot Shield - https://www.hotspotshield.com
Signal - https://whispersystems.org/
Smartphone Spy Apps -
http://www.hongkiat.com/blog/iphone-spy-apps/
Ear Spy - http://www.overpass.co.uk/app/ear-spy/
Ship Finder - http://shipfinder.co/about/
Tresorit - https://tresorit.com/
Seafile Secure Cloud Storage -
https://www.seafile.com/en/home/
FinSpy - https://wikileaks.org/spyfiles/files/0/289_GAMMA-
201110-FinSpy.pdf
Fake Tweets - http://www.lemmetweetthatforyou.com/
Expand Short Links - http://checkshorturl.com/
No More Ransom - https://www.nomoreransom.org/
Angry IP Scanner - http://angryip.org/
Shodan - https://www.shodan.io/
Philips HUE lighting system - http://www2.meethue.com
Mozilla Firefox - https://www.mozilla.org/en-US/firefox/new/
Firefox Add-Ons - https://addons.mozilla.org/en-US/firefox/
Open Office Suite - https://www.openoffice.org/
VLC media player - http://www.videolan.org/vlc/index.html
Foxit PDF Reader -
https://www.foxitsoftware.com/products/pdf-reader/
Recommended VPNs – https://www.deepdotweb.com/vpn-
comparison-chart/
Tor Onion Browser - https://www.torproject.org/
Evidence Nuker - http://www.evidencenuker.com/
AnonyMouse Email Remailer -
http://anonymouse.org/anonemail.html
Unseen Email - https://unseen.is/
PrivNote - https://privnote.com/#
PGP Pretty Good Privacy - http://www.pgpi.org/

Platform Operating System -
http://portableapps.com/download
Recommended Search Engines - https://duckduckgo.com/ and
see http://www.howtogeek.com/113513/5-alternative-search-
engines-that-respect-your-privacy/
Newsbin - http://www.newsbin.com/
Usenet - http://www.usenet.com/
OpenStego - http://www.openstego.com/
Deepdotweb - https://www.deepdotweb.com/
Hidden Wiki - https://thehiddenwiki.org/

Also recommended:
http://www.wonderhowto.com/

About the Author

Alan Pearce is a journalist, broadcaster and author with over 40 years' experience. He has written for Time magazine, The Sunday Times, The Times, The Sunday Telegraph and others, in addition to Sky News and various BBC outlets. He was injured covering the fall of Kabul in 1996 while working as the BBC's Afghanistan Correspondent and is the author of "Dunkirk Spirit", "Whose Side Are They On?", "The Google Questions" and the best-selling "Playing It Safe".

www.alanpearce.com
books@alanpearce.com

*

Special thanks to Ernest Sagaga, Head of Human Rights and Safety at the International Federation of Journalists, for his support, foresight and professionalism.

*

Made in the USA
Coppell, TX
27 February 2022

74184355R10069